BRIDGES

THEIR ART, SCIENCE AND EVOLUTION

CHARLES S. WHITNEY, M.C.E.

*Member of the American Institute of Consulting Engineers and
the American Society of Civil Engineers*

With a new foreword by Larry Spiller,
Executive Vice President,
American Consulting Engineers Council

ILLUSTRATED
WITH PHOTOGRAPHS AND DRAWINGS OF OLD
AND NEW BRIDGES OF MANY LANDS

GREENWICH HOUSE
DISTRIBUTED BY CROWN PUBLISHERS, INC.
NEW YORK

DEDICATED
TO THE MEMORY OF
THOSE PIONEER ENGINEERS
WHO CREATED BEAUTIFUL BRIDGES
TO JOIN TOGETHER THE
DEVIOUS PATHS
OF MEN

Copyright ©1983 by Greenwich House, a division of Arlington House, Inc.
All rights reserved.

This 1983 edition is published by Greenwich House, a division of Arlington
House, Inc., distributed by Crown Publishers, Inc.

Originally published as *Bridges: A Study in Their Art, Science and Evolution.*

Manufactured in the United States of America

Library of Congress Cataloging in Publication Data

Whitney, Charles S. (Charles Smith), 1892-1959
Bridges, their art, science, and evolution.

Reprint. Originally published: Bridges, a study in their art, science, and evolution.
New York : W.E. Rudge, 1929. Includes index.
1. Bridges.   I. Title.
TG15.W5   1983   624'.2   82-20972

ISBN: 0-517-402440
h g f e d c b a

CONTENTS

LIST OF ILLUSTRATIONS

PART ONE

Section v. *THE EIGHTEENTH CENTURY*

Section vi. *THE MODERN BRIDGE*

PART TWO

Section I. *INFLUENCE OF MATERIAL ON BRIDGE FORMS*

Section II. *BRIDGES OF WOOD*

SECTION III. *BRIDGES OF STONE*

FOREWORD

ALTHOUGH I never had the pleasure of meeting Charles S. Whitney in person, as I researched his background preparatory to the republication of *Bridges*, one central fact about the man emerged: Charles Whitney had a special appreciation, affection and awe for bridges. This is evident in the loving simplicity with which his 1929 book approaches the subject. Through diagrams and pictures, ranging from the Rainbow Natural Arch, "a bridge of living stone...[in] perfect union with the canyon walls," through history to the "remarkable" and "unprecedented" Roebling Brooklyn Bridge, Mr. Whitney's amazing collection of bridge photos all but tell their own story.

In a way, *Bridges: Their Art, Science and Evolution* tells Mr. Whitney's own story as well. As a young graduate civil engineer, his first employment was with a Los Angeles architect. After World War I he worked with an architect in Milwaukee. Thus, early in his career he gained an appreciation for melding the beauty of architecture with the stability of engineering. This appreciation carried over several years later as the principal theme of his historic book.

Whitney also recognized early that the most outstanding structures are not those built to exploit or exalt artistic or technological achievement but those built to further human welfare. During his thirty-seven-year career as a consulting structural engineer in Milwaukee and New York, he created predominantly people-oriented designs: bridges, churches, theaters, auditoria, airports, apartments and office buildings. And as he served the public, so also did he serve his profession.

Whitney traveled frequently from Milwaukee to New York to participate in meetings of the American Institute of Consulting Engineers (later to become the American Consulting Engineers Council). He was president, in 1955, of the American Concrete Institute, as well as an active member of the American Society of Civil Engineers which, in 1925, awarded him the James R. Croes Medal. Cornell University, from which he received his Masters in Civil Engineering, presented him with the Fuertes Graduate Medal in 1925 and again in 1927. In 1951 the American Concrete Institute selected him for the Alfred E. Lindau Award "in recognition of his many contributions to reinforced concrete design." In May 1959, just four months prior to his death, he was cited for his outstanding accomplishments at the 11th Annual Wisconsin Engineers Day celebration at the University of Wisconsin, which made special note of his work in the development of long-span, thin-shell concrete structures.

Charles Whitney was characterized by his one-time partner, Othar H. Amman (with whom he associated in 1946 to form the New York–based firm of Amman and Whitney), as "conservative, yet wary of conventional practice, and progressive in the development of new ideas." *Bridges: Their Art, Science and Evolution* is a perfect statement of those qualities; it also leaves little room for doubt that, regardless of size, material or location, bridges were Whitney's major passion. His superlatives for the genius of Caesar Augustus in building the Pons Augustus at Rimini, Italy, are as genuine as is his praise of Othar H. Amman's "ultimate in design achievement" — the 3,500-foot, main-span George Washington Bridge in New York City.

Somehow I doubt that Charles Whitney would be surprised were he to return today and see more recent bridges like the Humber and the Verrazano-Narrows, both with main spans approaching a mile in length. For he says it himself late in the book: "So rapid and complete was the development of the science of bridge engineering during the 19th century, that the 20th century engineer[is] well equipped to create the tremendous long-span bridges [of the future]."

Thanks to the editorial, historical and technical contributions of Charles S. Whitney, today's consulting structural engineers are, in fact, fulfilling that promise.

Larry N. Spiller
Executive Vice President
American Consulting Engineers Council

Washington, D.C.
1983

PREFACE

BRIDGES are among the most ancient and honorable members of society, with a background rich in tradition and culture. For countless generations they have borne the burdens of the world, and many of them have been great works of art. As in most large families, there are numerous poor relatives. The Modern Bridge too often appears as a workman performing its task for a minimum wage, mechanically efficient but uneducated and ignorant of its own ancestry. A worthy subject for serious consideration in this day of reform.

The purpose of this book is threefold. First: to give a method for the application of fundamental architectural principles to the design and criticism of bridges; to point out that the modern bridge should not, as is sometimes stated, be exempted from the same rules of art that apply to other architectural works; and to make a plea for thorough architectural training of the Civil Engineer that his tremendously important works may be as inspiringly beautiful as they are economically sound.

Second: to present the historical background of the Modern Bridge, showing how bridge building developed from the earliest time to the present day; how it has been influenced by social, political, and economic conditions; and picturing the most beautiful and interesting bridges of each period.

Third: to present a selection of photographs of artistic bridges of all types; which it is hoped will not only interest the layman but will furnish valuable inspiration to engineers and architects who are engaged in designing bridges. Not all of the designs pictured are to be considered as perfect, but they all have enough artistic merit to make their study worth while, and they show how their designers have solved the special problems involved.

The material for this book has been drawn from many sources. There is a considerable disagreement among various writers regarding the early history of bridges, and an attempt has been made to weigh authorities and select the most accurate information available. Degrand's "Ponts en Maçonnerie" and Viollet-le-Duc's "Dictionnaire Raisonné de l'Architecture" were drawn on heavily for the story of Roman and medieval bridges. DeDartein's "Études sur les Ponts en Maçonnerie" and Séjourné's "Grandes Voûtes" furnished much of the information on later bridges of masonry. Other sources are referred to in the text.

The source of the photographs is acknowledged under each illustration. The author wishes especially to express his deep appreciation of assistance given him by Paul Séjourné, Ingénieur en Chef des Ponts et Chaussées; Adolf Bühler, Bridge Engineer, National Swiss Railways; and Dr. Ing. Fritz Emperger, who have greatly helped in the difficult task of collecting suitable photographs; and by Alexander C. Eschweiler, F.A.I.A., and Carl F. Eschweiler, A.I.A., who have advised in the selection and preparation of material. He also wishes to thank the many others who have furnished material or have given suggestions and encouragement which have made the task a very pleasant one.

C.S.W.

PART I · SECTION I

ART AND SCIENCE IN BRIDGE DESIGN

ART AND SCIENCE IN BRIDGE DESIGN

FAR flung across a wide river, defying the elements, resisting the law of gravity, and carrying an endless stream of human life above the tops of the tallest ships, a great bridge is the triumph of modern science. Who is not thrilled and inspired by the skill of the builder? And how many realize that as deep as the foundations of the bridge carried down to bed rock far below the river, so deep are the foundations of the science of bridge building, extending back to the very beginning of civilization?

Bridges typify progress more than any other structures built by man. They span obstructions in his path and open new routes of communication. As need increases, they are thrown across wider rivers and deeper valleys. Considered from the beginning, the growth of bridge building seems almost biological, sometimes accelerated by fertile civilization and sometimes blighted by barbarism. The bridge engineer acts as agent in this evolution of the bridge. He is directed by economic conditions over which he has no control, and he is himself a product of these conditions. In the early days, he was an architect unhampered by the complexity into which building operations have since fallen. He built structures so that they appeared correct to his eye. If they fell, he rebuilt them with sturdier proportions. The results were more pleasing in appearance than many of the coldly scientific modern bridges. In this way were built the marvelous Roman aqueducts and bridges, the picturesque medieval spans and the beautiful masterpieces of the Renaissance.

During the eighteenth century, following the Renaissance period, the civilized countries became so well organized that public works were undertaken on a large scale. France began the construction of a comprehensive system of highways and canals; and to help in this work, an engineering school was organized in Paris. A similar development took place in England. This extensive engineering work allowed the engineers less time to study or practice architecture. Bridges became more scientific, but beautiful designs were still produced because of the influence of the older work.

The next important influence on the evolution of bridges was the building of railroads in the nineteenth century. The railroads required great bridges which could be built cheaply and quickly. Especially in America, conditions necessitated the construction of the greatest possible number of bridges at minimum cost. The modern engineer has been influenced by these

conditions; and being so trained, usually he has no more ability for artistic expression than the layman. Fortunately, these conditions are gradually being modified. Capital has been accumulated in quantities which warrant the construction of permanent artistic bridges, and the bridge engineer will be trained to meet the demand. With the assistance of architects, many beautiful bridges have been built in recent years; but it must also be admitted that, in many cases, even the cooperation of engineer and architect has not been successful. The architect is generally as untrained in bridge design as the engineer is in art, so that sympathetic and intelligent collaboration is often impossible.

Since the seventeenth century, the science of bridge building has progressed more rapidly than the art. So complete in itself is modern science and so rapid has been its development within the last few generations, that the engineer does not need to look back of recent experience to build strong and economical bridges. Because the materials and methods now used are so different from those of even a hundred years ago, the modern bridge engineer has paid little attention to the works of previous centuries which have made the modern bridge possible. Today, the engineer finds himself heir to a great wealth of experience gradually accumulated by his predecessors, one development having led to several, ramifying like the branches of a tree. The roots of this tree were grown long ago when elementary principles of the beam, the arch, and the suspension system were discovered. Every bridge design is based on one or more of these principles.

The scientists have wrought miracles and deserve great credit for their success. But actually what is science to a bridge, except as a means to an end? Bridges are built to further human welfare and not to exploit or exalt scientific principles. Such principles should not be allowed to control the outward form too rigidly for they are of particular interest only to the scientist himself. The development of science is recent, but the methods of artistic expression appear to have been as well understood by the Romans as they are today. The fundamental principles of art were the same then as now. They apply alike to the ancient stone bridge, the medieval cathedral, and the modern steel bridge. Materials and forms change but the principles of art remain the same. Architectural styles which conflict with such principles are only temporary fads.

Beauty is a thing apart from human progress. The old bridges themselves still form the most valuable treatise on the art of bridge design. They were built with a simplicity and sincerity which it is difficult to duplicate in this sophisticated age. These worthy veterans reflect the glory of empires, and their story is as dramatic as the political history with which it is so closely connected.

Before continuing with the biography of the bridge, let us first consider the form of its anatomy. An understanding of the general principles of bridge design will permit a sympathetic study of the development of the bridge through the ages.

A bridge may form a charming picture, with perhaps a view of meadow and river meeting, people passing over, light playing above with mysterious shadows and reflections below, currents eddying and rippling about the piers and sparkling in the sunlight. Or it may stride across the sky from cliff to cliff high above a mountain stream. Yet, with all the natural advantages, some bridges are discordant. The reasons are worth investigating.

If a number of men were asked to measure the length of a bridge, their answers would

PHOTO BY EWING GALLOWAY

PLATE I. Blackwell's Island and Lower Manhattan under the Queensboro Bridge

[25]

PLATE 2. The Hudson River Suspension Bridge at New York. Preliminary Drawing of the World's Greatest Span. 3500 feet between centers of towers. *O. H. Ammann, Chief Engineer. Cass Gilbert, Consulting Architect.*

[26]

agree quite closely. If they attempted to measure beauty, the replies would all be different. Beauty is an indefinite, elusive quality. It depends not on what a thing is but what it appears to be. A thing of beauty by moonlight may be hideous as revealed during the day. When artists and professional critics cannot agree, how is the layman to judge the merits of a design?

In matters of art, there is no definite authority to which to turn. There are, however, certain rules which may be used to measure the adequacy of a bridge. Even though the results vary with the experience and training of the person who uses them, these rules permit a logical analysis and lead to the formation of definite opinions. Each person may decide at least to his own satisfaction why one design pleases the eye and another does not.

There are a number of books on the principles of architectural design which should be very interesting to bridge engineers. The application of these principles to bridge design can be but briefly outlined here; but it is hoped that this outline will encourage further study. The subject is not a new one. About two thousand years ago, a Roman architect, Vitruvius, hoping to win fame and fortune, wrote ten books on architecture* which he addressed to Caesar. In order to impress his Emperor with his superior knowledge, he discussed many scientific subjects allied with his profession. Naïve as his ideas of science now seem, his remarks on professional relations apply with startling accuracy to present practice. He also gave considerable information on the origin and use of Greek and Roman architectural forms.

In the sixteenth century, Palladio, an Italian architect, explained the bridge in the following way: "The convenience of bridges was first thought upon because many rivers are not fordable by reasons of their largeness, depth, and rapidity: upon which account it may be well said, that bridges are a principal part of the way; and are nothing else but a street or way continued over water. Bridges therefore ought to have the self-same qualifications that are judged requisite in all other fabricks: which are, that they shall be convenient, beautiful and durable." That paragraph states the fundamental principle of bridge design. In addition to being strong and convenient, the bridge should be beautiful and should express the fact that it is but a part of a continuous street or way.

There seems to be a general agreement among those who have expressed opinions on the subject, although the opinions are variously stated, that an ideal bridge must possess two general qualities. These are structural efficiency and unity of appearance. This latter term requires considerable explanation; and even the obvious sounding "structural efficiency," which will first be discussed, is not as simple as it seems.

Structural considerations require that the material of the bridge shall be so proportioned

* "Vitruvius, The Ten Books on Architecture," translated by Morris Hicky Morgan. Harvard University Press.

and placed as to provide convenience and durability. The width and arrangement of roadway and waterway should suit the needs of traffic. The construction should be strong enough to stand safely as long as it is wanted. But structural efficiency means much more than convenience and durability at the least cost. It means providing convenience, durability, and *beauty* by the simplest and most direct means. Beauty does not demand elaborate ornamentation, and is not in any way opposed to efficiency. Beauty is in fact so closely related to efficiency that it sometimes seems to result entirely from perfect fitness. Consider the beauty of the gracefully curved ax handle whose form is fixed by utility. No ornamentation is needed there. And what is more beautiful than the simple curve of a Roman arch?

Strength, although it is absolutely necessary, is to some extent a negative virtue. We cannot judge by the appearance of a structure whether it actually has sufficient strength, but we know that if it is deficient in strength it will collapse. Strength is invisible when present and conspicuous only in its absence. On the contrary, beauty, which in itself demands an appearance of strength, gives pleasure wherever it is found. A weak bridge is admittedly more dangerous than an ugly one, but to seek strength at the lowest cost with no regard for appearance is only one degree worse than it would be to attempt a beautiful design without thought of stability.

The bridge must not only be durable, but it should have the appearance of strength so that it may be used with confidence. To this end, the manner in which the loads are carried to the abutments and piers should be obvious to the eye, although it is not necessary for the labor of every member to be apparent. A mere suggestion of the method of support may be enough. The load should be carried as easily and gracefully as possible. The great arch which struts across the sky with much show of strength and bracing is less pleasing than the bridge whose arch calmly rests below the roadway. The suspension bridge with its graceful, slender cables is more attractive than the heavy, long-span braced arch.

Although the appearance of stability is of great importance when the bridge is seen from the side, the interest of the person using the

PLATE 3. Chertsey Bridge over the Thames, England.

PLATE 4. Landwasser Viaduct of the Albula-Bahn, Switzerland

bridge is somewhat different. He sees nothing below the roadway and does not care to see much of anything above it. A partial view of the structural system, visible when the trusses or arches extend above the roadway, is apt to be neither reassuring nor beautiful. The roadways of some bridges intersect the structures in such a way that only a meaningless portion of framing is visible to the passer-by. It would be better to allow him to forget the effort the bridge is making and enjoy the open landscape spread before him. The through truss bridge is appropriate for only one kind of service, and that is for railroad trains. An iron cage for an iron monster. Steelwork flashing by the car window is rather comforting when one is passing high over a river with no visible means of support below.

Structural efficiency also demands that materials be used logically in forms made suitable by their particular characteristics. Because of the variety of materials, it has often happened in modern work that one has been substituted for another without properly modifying the form. Whenever a new material is introduced, instead of taking advantage of its peculiar properties, there is a tendency to build it into the familiar shapes determined by the nature of the material formerly used. The designer should realize that no material can be used efficiently in forms especially suitable to another. Even the various kinds of stone are so different from each other that the details appropriate to one may not be used for another. The delicate carving of marble should not be attempted in granite.

Concrete blocks cast in the form of quarry-faced stone are hideous, yet cast stone is a material which has many good qualities. It can be made so that it will be pleasing in appearance and satisfactory in service, and its use is justified when it is formed and finished appropriately. A material is selected for use because of certain appropriate qualities it possesses, and it should always be so used as to express itself rather than some other material. That is why monolithic concrete should not be marked with joints to represent stone masonry, although it may be desirable to use some lines to add interest to large plain surfaces, or to indicate construction joints. Plate 5 shows a well designed bridge which expresses concrete in a very interesting way.

The principle of efficiency applies in the same way to the general appearance of the bridge. When one type of structure is chosen because of its fitness, it should not represent another type. It might improve the appearance to curve the bottom of a beam somewhat in the form of an arch, but that would not be the same as marking the face of the beam to represent arch stones. Efficiency is concerned with what a bridge does and how it performs its task. Suitability and fitness may have nearly the same meaning as efficiency, if considered in a broad sense. If the bridge performs its duties in a direct and graceful manner, it will have no oppor-

Plate 5. Hijiri-Bashi, Built by the Reconstruction Bureau in Tokyo, 1924

tunity to hide behind false faces. It cannot be efficient if it imitates. Whatever it is, it must face the world truthfully and without shame or sham.

Some of the advocates of truthfulness in architecture have become so radical that they are difficult to please. Since the introduction of the steel-frame skyscraper, they have worried because such structures are covered with masonry instead of exposing only steelwork, rivets, and glass so that all who walk may read. They object to such practice as covering steel or concrete structures with stone for fear that some one passing may not know what is inside of them. They are not willing to admit that a masonry covering for the steel frame of a large building is logical because even if exposed steel is protected from rust by perpetually repeated painting, the change in temperature from summer sun to winter frost will cause serious difficulties from expansion and contraction because of lack of insulation. It is difficult to see how such objections are justified if the construction is fundamentally logical and sound. A stone covering for steel or concrete may sometimes be proper to protect it from the elements or to provide a harmonious architectural treatment. Obviously, its use could be abused if stonework were constructed only as a sham serving no structural purpose. It is no more necessary for us to see the material inside of a bridge than it is to look through the bark of a tree.

The Romans built bridge and aqueduct piers with a stone or brick shell filled with concrete; but the shell served as a form for the concrete, and the concrete was of such quality that it did not have sufficient strength to carry the loads alone and needed protection from the weather. Granite facing is also properly used on modern piers because granite will stand severe exposure better than concrete.

Palladio's three requisites for a well-behaved bridge were convenience, beauty, and durability. He even had the courage to mention beauty before durability, but he had never seen the crowds seething across a twentieth century bridge. As far as convenience and durability are concerned, no one need argue with the modern bridge engineer. Beauty has not been the forte of the scientist but it is not beyond his reach. It is not subject to mathematical calculation, but neither is it hopelessly indeterminate. It is really more a matter of fitness than ornamentation, not a luxury to be enjoyed only by favored bridges.

The bridge is part of a roadway which it carries across an obstacle. Since a part cannot be greater than the whole, the bridge should not be made to appear more important than the road itself or the river banks between which it establishes communication. The bridge is usually dominated by the landscape or buildings, and its proper architectural treatment is determined by its relations with its surroundings. It should always be designed so that it fits gracefully into the picture without being overbearing or too conspicuous.

This leads to a consideration of unity of appearance which was mentioned with structural efficiency as being one of the qualities necessary to the ideal bridge. A bridge which possesses unity in all respects, whose parts are harmonious and which is in harmony with its surroundings, must be pleasing to see. Simplicity is also a real aid to beauty because it is so closely related

PHOTO FRATELLI ALINARI

PLATE 6. Ponte di San Francesco, San Remo, Italy

PLATE 7. Rainbow Natural Arch, Utah

to unity. Through a study of unity a number of facts may be discovered which will be helpful in bridge design.

Since the bridge is a part of its setting and is itself composed of a number of parts, there are two phases of unity, external and internal. External unity involves the relations between the bridge and all around it, land, road, water, buildings, other bridges, and even the hills and valley. Internal unity is oneness of the bridge itself and depends only on the relation between the different parts of the bridge.

External unity is first to be considered. The single span of the Rainbow Natural Arch, a bridge of living stone sprung between cliffs of the same substance, presents a perfect union with the canyon walls (Plate 7). Likewise, the greatest charm of many of the old stone bridges is due to the use of only one material, the local stone which has aged and mellowed, blending the bridge with the landscape. This effect cannot be fully obtained with steel and concrete, but among other steel and concrete structures these materials may not seem incongruous. A steel girder bridge may seem appropriate when carrying a steel railroad track. In securing unity, harmony of materials in texture and color is very important. Stonework

[33]

PLATE 8. Ponte Vittorio Emanuele II, Rome. *T. Capriati and Enr. De Rossi, Engineers*

PLATE 9. Harmoniously Designed Bridge over the Danube at Münderkingen, Württemberg. 1893

[34]

which may be rough for country bridges should be dressed and smoothed to some degree when placed in cities. Formal, elaborate designs demand a formal background. Due to the ornateness of its treatment, the white marble arches of the Ponte Vittorio Emanuele II appear entirely out of place between the old embankments of the Tiber, under the shadow of Hadrian's Tomb (Plate 8). Such an ostentatious bridge should never have been placed near the dignified Roman arches of the venerable Pons Aelius.

Modern designers too frequently make the similar mistake of applying too much ornament to bridges in the open country. Elaborately cast concrete railings and mouldings are placed on bridges in the mountains or forests where the traveler wants only to be allowed to enjoy nature unimproved. This is probably done with the good intention of making the bridges worthy of their beautiful natural settings. Unfortunately, most of the ornamentation is not well designed; but even if it were, the effect would be a disconcerting competition with the beauties of nature. Such competition is bad taste and is sure to be unsuccessful. A very simple architectural treatment is more effective in natural surroundings.

City bridges may be more formal in design, but they should always recognize the importance of other nearby structures. They should be as nearly as possible in scale with the neighboring bridges and buildings, with spans neither so small as to appear trivial nor so large as to be overbearing.

The points of contact between the bridge and the land and water should be studied and so designed that the bridge will be properly related to the river and its banks. The roadway extends beyond the end of the bridge and this continuity should be expressed at the abutments. Instead of ending abruptly at the bank, the bridge may be connected with the land by appropriately-shaped walls directed to lead the traffic onto the spans. At the ends of many of the old bridges, plazas were built and sometimes the end spans themselves were flared out to form a transition.

The water forms a base for the visible part of the bridge and a horizontal tie between the pier bases parallel to the roadway. Piers should be provided with base and cutwater, properly recognizing the water line. In tidal waters, or rivers subject to considerable fluctuation of water level, it is very important to study the appearance of the piers at both high and low water. If proper provision is not made, the bridge may appear stilted at low water or dangerously submerged at high water.

Turning now to unity of the internal variety, we will consider the relations between the various parts of the bridge itself. When stone was the only material used for permanent bridges, unity resulted naturally to a considerable degree. A bridge was built of a uniform

PLATE 10. Alfred H. Smith Memorial Bridge, Carrying the New York Central Railway across the Hudson River at Castleton, N. Y. An example of lack of unity due to practical limitations.

PLATE 11. The Old Bridge at Tours, France, by Bayeux and de Volgie. 1764–77. Unity secured by repetition of similar spans.

PLATE 12. The Eighteenth Century Bridge at Blois, France, by Gabriel. 1716–24. Individuality through emphasis of central span.

PLATE 13. The Pont de la Coulouvrenière over the Rhone at Geneva, Switzerland. 1896. An example of duality. *C. Butticaz, Engineer; M. Bouvier, Architect.*

material in its entirety. All of the spans were arches, and the arches and piers were proportioned by eye instead of by mathematical calculations. At the present time, many other materials are available for use in many forms. The necessity for building cheap bridges has often resulted in the combination of parts which are entirely unrelated to each other in form and material. Piers of steel and piers of concrete, steel trusses of various forms, steel girders and concrete spans are placed together without regard for unity of appearance.

The requirements of internal unity may be summarized as follows: individuality, continuity, balance, similarity of parts, proportion, scale, and harmony in color and texture of materials.

Individuality has a meaning somewhat similar to that of unity itself, but more restricted in sense. It is a characteristic opposed to duality or multiplicity, involving principally the number of parts. It requires that there be only one major part to which all others are subordinated. This may be accomplished in a bridge by making the center span longer and higher than those on either side. Strictly speaking, unity may result from either individuality or continuity, but both should be provided in an architectural composition if possible. The old bridge at Tours (Plate 11) with its series of equal spans possesses unity and continuity, but lacks the individuality of the bridge at Blois (Plate 12). If possible, there should always be a focal point to which the eye is led and allowed to rest. At Blois, there were eleven spans increasing in length with the roadway sloping up to the focal point at the center of the bridge where the cartouches and obelisque are placed.

If there are two or more equal spans, the eye wanders back and forth, making comparisons instead of being drawn to the center of the composition. However, in the case of a very long bridge or viaduct, continuity becomes relatively more important and it is not practicable to secure individuality through the dominance of one of the spans. The bridges at Blois and Tours are interesting examples of the two methods of treatment.

PLATE 14. The Old Pont de la Gare at Lyon, France. 1831. Duality in a two-span bridge offset by the emphasis on the central pier.

PLATE 15. Pont Morand at Lyon, France. 1890. *H. Girardon, Ing. en Chef; H. Cavernier, Ing. Ord.* Continuity of railing broken by change of material.

PLATE 16. Bridge at Saint-André-de Cubzac, France. Continuity in a steel truss bridge

A multiple span bridge is divided into a number of parts by the piers; and, in general, especially if the number of spans is less than seven, it is better to have a span at the center rather than a pier. Using an odd number of spans avoids duality and permits the placing of one dominant span at the center. Palladio showed his appreciation of this principle when he wrote: "The pilasters, which are made according to the largeness of the river, ought to be of an even number; as well because we feel that nature produced from this number all those things which, consisting of more than one part, are to bear any weight, as the feet of man and all animals may convince us: as likewise because such compartment is more beautiful to look upon and renders the work stronger, since the course of the river in the middle (in which place it is naturally most rapid for being farthest from the banks) is there free and does not endanger the pilasters by continually shaking them." Palladio does not say why such compartment is more beautiful to look upon and his logic is quaint, but he correctly felt the propriety of such an arrangement of spans.

Continuity is a requirement of unity for which there are obvious reasons. Being a part of a continuous roadway and being itself comparatively long and narrow, a bridge should proceed with a certain continuous stride or rhythm across the water, avoiding abrupt changes in the spans and pronounced breaks in the line of the roadway. The high-humped Devil's Bridge near Lucca (Plate 70) and the zig-zag bridge at Besalú (Plate 76) represent types which have no place in modern life because they would be useless for swift-moving traffic. The bridge is divided horizontally into parts by the piers, which are usually accented by architectural features, such as lamps or even statues. Such accenting is desirable, but if it is overdone there is danger of breaking the continuity of the design. This interruption frequently occurs when the spans and the piers are of different materials, as when light steel or iron arches are carried on masonry piers. This fault is slightly noticeable in the Pont Morand at Lyons (Plate 15), and also, because of over-emphasis of the piers, in the Ponte Vittorio Emanuele II in Rome. Lack of continuity appears in the typical American steel truss railroad bridge with inclined end posts, leaving a gap in the line of the top chords at the piers. This defect has been overcome in European practice by keeping the top and bottom chords continuous and parallel from one end to the other (Plate 16).

Because bridges are comparatively long and narrow, continuous horizontal lines must dominate the design. In the piers themselves, on the contrary, the vertical dimension is usually greater than the horizontal; and if the verticality of the piers is too strongly emphasized, the continuous horizontal sweep of the bridge will be broken. It is interesting to note how the piers of the Ponte S. Trinita have been capped just below the parapet for this very

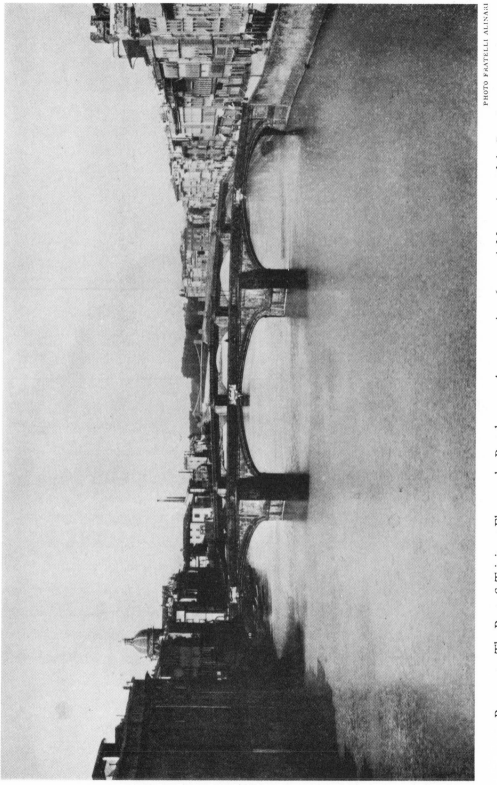

PLATE 17. The Ponte S. Trinita at Florence, by Bartolommeo Ammannati. 1567-70. A Masterpiece of the Renaissance

reason (Plate 17). Contrast with this the strong vertical lines of the Pont Valentré at Cahors (Plate 61), whose three fortified towers were built to make the passage of enemies as difficult as possible. This bridge expresses its medieval function as perfectly as the Ponte S. Trinita reflects the spirit of the Renaissance, but it lacks the unity of the latter bridge.

Some bridges, such as the Pont du Gard and the Segovian aqueduct, have been divided into parts vertically as well as horizontally (Plates 44 and 46). The Pont du Gard has three tiers, the middle one being the tallest. In the Segovian Aqueduct, the lower tier is much taller than the upper. As a general rule, there should never be a division into more than three major parts vertically, and one of these must be given more importance than the other two. This triple division corresponds somewhat with the base, shaft, and capital of a column.

When it is possible, the design should be balanced about the center or about the focal point of the composition. This does not necessitate exact symmetry, but an unsymmetrical design should be avoided unless there is apparent reason for it.

The principle of similarity is also one which is frequently violated in modern bridges. Ordinarily, those parts of the bridge which perform the same function should be similar in form. The combination of girders, arches, and trusses for the main spans of a bridge should be avoided. The use of arches of different shapes may add interest to a medieval structure, because it tells a story of intermittent building or reconstruction; but it would not be easily excused in well-planned modern work. If it is necessary to use one type of span for the approach and another for the main bridge, the approach spans should be so subordinated and separated that they do not conflict with the principal ones.

Opposing similarity, contrast between parts not performing the same function, may be used for emphasis. Straight lines in the piers and roadway contrast with the curve of the arch, and carved ornaments are always made more effective by contrast with plain surfaces.

Proportion and scale depend on relative dimensions and not on absolute size. The thickness of a pier compared with its height or length may be considered its proportion. For proper appearance, the proportions of all piers of a bridge should be similar if they carry similar loads and those carrying heavier loads should be proportionately heavier. The same is true of the spans. If one part of a bridge is too large or too small compared with most of the other parts, it is said to be out of scale.

The size or scale of ornamentation should be regulated according to the distance from which it will be seen. Large scale ornaments tend to have a heavy appearance or to reduce the apparent size of the bridge, depending on whether they are seen from a near or distant point. Thus, large statues on the rail of a bridge may look colossal from the roadway; but if

PLATE 18. The Pons Aelius at Rome, with Seventeenth Century Statues and Railings

viewed from the river, they make the bridge appear smaller by comparison. The scale of ornamental features must be carefully studied. In general, ornaments to be seen from the river in a side view of the bridge should be in scale with the entire bridge, and those seen from the roadway should be in scale with the railing and the people. Hence, large statues may be placed at the pier ends below the railing, but when set above the rail they should be smaller. It may be noticed that there is a conflict here because statues above the rail may be seen from both the roadway and the river.

This leads to another question which has caused considerable controversy. Should statues placed above the railing be faced toward the river to enhance the general view of the bridge, and turn their backs toward all those who use the bridge; or should they face the roadway and spurn those observers for whom the beauty of the bridge itself is really created? A bridge has this peculiarity, that those who use it can see only the railing and roadway, and not the general form of the bridge. The answer to this question is difficult, for it depends entirely on the nature of the bridge and its surroundings. If the bridge is ornamented principally to beautify a river basin the statues may be turned out, but usually they are faced toward the roadway to honor the passer-by. In any case, it would seem that statues facing the river should be large ones in scale with the bridge itself. If they face the roadway, their size should be de-

PLATE 19. Well Designed Statuary on a Pier of the Wittelsbacherbrücke, Munich, Germany. 1905. *Prof. Theodore Fischer, Architect; Saget & Woerner, Engineers.*

termined by the width and importance of the roadway and the distance from which they may be seen by the people passing.

There are many examples to be studied. On the Pons Aelius in Rome, large statues are placed above the railing facing the narrow roadway and they have the effect of dwarfing the bridge (Plate 18). The equestrian statue on the Wittelsbacherbrücke in Munich is very well designed (Plate 19). High above the roadway which it faces, it is seen almost equally from the road and the river. When seen from a distance with the bridge, it is only part of the large monument formed by the pedestal on the pier end. The size of the single figure on the Maximiliansbrücke in Munich (Plate 20) may be justified by the width of the roadway, but if a number of such figures were placed along the bridge the effect would certainly be similar to that on the Pons Aelius.

Perhaps the question regarding the placing of the statues on bridges could best be answered by removing them entirely and placing them on separate pedestals at the entrance to the bridge, so that they form a part of the roadway approach and do not conflict with the general view of the bridge. The view of the Prinzregentenbrücke shows how satisfactory this treatment can be (Plate 22). Statues at the pier ends just above the water do not seem appropriate, especially when they are partly submerged by floods, as are the unfortunate poilus on the Pont de l'Alma in Paris. Considerable criticism has been directed toward the placing on the pier ends of any ornaments borrowed from civic architecture, such as columns which have no meaning in that location.

Attractive as the towers, triumphal arches, and pylons of the old bridges may be, such features should be used with great caution in new bridges, and never unless they serve a real purpose. Defensive towers were built for reasons which no longer exist. Nothing can justify meaningless construction on a bridge.

Bridge railings may be designed in many attractive forms, solid or light appearing as

PLATE 20. The Maximiliansbrücke, Munich, Germany. 1903–05. *Prof. Theodore Fischer, Architect; Saget & Woerner, Engineers.*

PLATE 21. The Roadway of the Maximiliansbrücke, Munich

PLATE 22. Prinzregentenbrücke, Munich, Germany. 1901. *Saget & Woerner, Engineers; Prof. Theodore Fischer, Architect.*

[46]

PHOTO COURTESY OF FRANK BARBER AND R. C. HARRIS

PLATE 23. Concrete Railing of Bloor Street Viaduct, Toronto, Canada. *Designed and Built by the City of Toronto Works Department.*

PHOTO FROM FRANK BARBER

PLATE 24. Concrete Handrail with Colored Encaustic Tile Inserts. East York-Leaside Viaduct, Toronto, Canada. *Frank Barber, Engineer; Claude Bragdon, Consulting Architect.*

desired. The use of one material for the rail on the spans and another on the piers is often unfortunate, as there should be an appearance of continuity from one end of the bridge to the other. Iron, bronze, cut stone, concrete or cast stone, terra cotta, and brick have all been used very successfully. Attractive handrails have been built of concrete with polychrome faience tile inserts. The rail is about the only ornamental part of the bridge which can be seen from the roadway, and its design is very important.

[47]

PLATE 25. Glazed Faience Panels Set in Concrete Handrail, Hunter Street Bridge, Peterborough, Canada. *Frank Barber, Engineer; Claude Bragdon, Architect.*

PLATE 26. Cast Stone Balusters for Bridge Railing, Washington, D. C.

The principles which have been explained should be helpful in forming a method of criticism of bridge designs, but they are not definite enough to permit design by rule. They will help to locate faults and form a standard of comparison. The creation of good designs requires natural ability and taste, and a thorough training involving much study and practice. The bridge engineer has had a thorough scientific training, but he must become a serious student

PLATE 27. Stone Bridge in North Wales

of architecture. The results obtained on many bridges on which both architects and engineers have been engaged, indicates that cooperation between an architect and an engineer, respectively untrained in bridge engineering and architecture, does not assure a proper blending of art and science.

The bridge is essentially an engineering structure. Utility imposes only one condition, that the bridge provide a convenient roadway, and this condition does not determine how the roadway shall be carried. The form of a building is fixed by the use to which it is put; but in the case of the bridge, other considerations such as depth and width of waterway, navigation requirements, the height of the roadway above the water, the character of the foundations and the land available for abutments or anchorages, are the ones which control the general form. The evaluation of these conditions so as to produce an efficient bridge is distinctly an engineering problem. Even the best design is a compromise and it may not be as beautiful as might seem desirable. The bridge engineer trained in the principles of architectural design will still feel the need of the assistance of an able architect. The day of the self-sufficient master-builder has passed.

PART I · SECTION II

THE ROMAN GENIUS

PHOTO BY JUDGES, LTD.

PLATE 28. Ancient Clapper Bridge, Postbridge, Dartmoor, England

PHOTO BY JUDGES, LTD.

PLATE 29. Ancient Clapper Bridge, Dartmeet, England

SECTION TWO

THE ROMAN GENIUS

THE art of constructing bridges dates back to the most remote antiquity. Its origin may have been man's first attempt to control the forces of nature. The first bridges were natural ones of stone or fallen trees. These were imitated by primitive man as soon as he developed the necessary tools and equipment. He could not have failed to observe some form of natural bridge and so did not have the opportunity to originate the idea himself. He may have started by felling a tree across a watercourse. Later such timbers were cut and fashioned to suit his convenience. The next development may have followed the idea of stepping-stones which suggested placing piers between the banks of wider streams with separate spans between. Primitive suspension bridges were also built of vines. Gradually more complex forms were evolved.

In his commentaries, Caesar mentions timber bridges which he found in Gaul having the appearance of antique constructions. The piers were built of trunks of trees placed in regular layers at right angles to each other with the center filled with stones. Above the piers the layers of tree projected further and further over the water, until they met and formed a sort of ogival arch. The roadway was formed of a layer of smaller timbers laid crosswise. The bridge in Cashmere, India, shown in Plate 31 follows this type but the piers are farther apart and are connected by spans of logs. The timber cantilever bridges of Bhutan are somewhat similar, but of more highly developed form which may also have been used in very ancient times (Plates 32, 225 and 226).

Records of very early bridges are all vague. According to the translation of Amyot, Diodorus of Sicily spoke of a bridge across the Euphrates at Babylon built by Queen Semiramis about 2000 B.C. The piers were said to be about twelve feet apart and built of stones fastened together with large iron bars anchored into holes with lead. They were founded in deep water and at the up-stream ends were constructed with triangular points of masonry to fend off the current and protect the bridge from the force of the water. The roadway was built of beams and planks of cedar, cypress, and palm. The manner of the construction of this bridge is evidence that even at this time the art of bridge building was not in its infancy. This work was completed in the presence of a great number of architects and workmen, whom Semiramis had called together from all parts of the known world to aid in its construction, so it may

PLATE 30. Rainbow Natural Arch, Utah

PLATE 31. Timber Bridge in Cashmere, India

[55]

PHOTO BY JOHN C. WHITE

Plate 32. Timber Cantilever Bridge in Bhutan, India

be assumed that the art of constructing such bridges was known in all countries. These were of timber with stone or timber piers.

The arch of stone may have been a later development. Some writers have assumed that the stone arch was first suggested by natural arches of stone. That is not so certain, because there is no reason why a monolithic stone arch or the curved ceiling of a cave would suggest the arching of several separate stones. The structural principles of the natural bridge and the man-made stone arch are quite different. It is easier to understand how prehistoric man may have noticed that one stone wedged between two others was supported by the pressure from their sides and that two or more stones could be supported in the same way. Once the principle was appreciated, the natural arches would form models which could be imitated.

In Egypt, Greece, and Asia Minor examples of very ancient stone arches have been found, built with horizontal joints, the stones projecting further and further until they met at the top (Plate 33). Similar ancient arches have been found in Mexico. In some of the pyramids of Egypt and Ethiopia, true arches laid with stone or brick with converging joints prove that this method of construction was known at least eighteen centuries before Christ. It seems strange that, if the Greeks and Egyptians had known how to build arches, they should have used the much heavier and more expensive horizontal beam construction in practically all of

PLATE 33. Primitive Form of Arch

PLATE 34. The Island in the Tiber, Rome. Pons Senatorius or "Ponte Rotto" in the foreground and the Pons Cestius and Pons Fabricus in the background.

their architecture. The arch could not have been unknown because Aristotle spoke of arch keystones which support the construction by the "resistance which they oppose to all parts." In his "Traité d'Architecture," M. Léonce Reynaud says: "It is without doubt necessary to attribute the small influence which it has exercised on the architecture of the two peoples to an exaggerated respect for consecrated forms."

It is possible that stone bridges were built in very ancient times but that through lack of careful maintenance they were destroyed so that no trace remains. The most ancient bridges which have survived to the present time are those built by the Romans. The great age of Roman bridge building started about 300 years before the Birth of Christ. The skill of the builders developed so rapidly that as early as the second century before Christ they produced bridges whose beauty of form and excellence of construction have not yet been surpassed.

This remarkable work continued until the end of the second century after Christ, when it commenced to decline. After the middle of the fourth century, the Roman art was lost. The Empire of the Orient, in spite of the magnificence of its capital and the grandeur which it imported from Rome, never built any bridges which were more than poor imitations of the Roman work. It was not until the pointed or ogival arches, originated in Persia, had succeeded the Roman style that monuments of real value were built in Constantinople and different parts of the Eastern Empire. Those belong to the medieval period.

Probably the first architects familiar with the construction of arches came to Rome from Etruria and built the first vaulted sewers and arched aqueducts. According to some authors, Tarquin was of Etruscan origin. In any case, he spent several years subjugating Etruria to the Roman rule, and it is probable that he took back to Rome with him architects and skilled workmen to execute the public works which he contemplated. The Cloaca-Maxima, supposed to be the oldest of the vaulted sewers, was built during Tarquin's reign, about 600 B.C. It was a work of great importance at the time and consisted of a considerable length of semi-circular barrel-vault nearly twenty feet in diameter. It was also during this time that the Pons Solarus, the oldest bridge attributed to the Romans, was built over the Teverone, a tributary of the Tiber. This bridge was destroyed a number of times and no definite information exists as to its original design.

It was in connection with the construction of aqueducts that the use of arches became common practice. The first of these is the Marcia aqueduct which brought water to Rome from the Apennines, about fifty-seven miles away. The canal was carried over the ravines and valleys on bridges and arcades more than six miles in length. These structures were built, it is said, about 145 B.C. and their ruins are among the most magnificent of the Roman Campagna.

PLATE 35. The Pons Fabricus, Rome. Built or repaired by Fabricus about 63 B.C.

The first bridge of ancient Rome of which there is any record, is the Pons Sublicus which was held by Horatius Cocles and two companions against the whole Etruscan army under Porsena. There is no definite information as to its construction or its location beyond the fact that it was a wooden bridge resting on piles, built during the reign of Ancus Marcius between 640 and 616 B.C.

The most ancient bridges which still exist in Rome are proof of the rapidity and completeness with which the Romans developed the art of bridge construction. The oldest of these is the Pons Senatorius or Pons Palatinus which was constructed about 181 B.C. It still stood in 1575 almost intact, when it was restored by Gregory XIII. A few years later, in 1598, all but one span was carried away by an exceptional flood and it has since been known as the Ponte Rotto, or "broken bridge" (Plate 34). The arches were semicircular with a span of eighty feet. The piers were about twenty-six feet thick, and were finished with angular cut-waters at each end, above which were arranged niches between two pilasters carrying the cornice. In the spandrels were carved dolphins. The design was harmonious and in excellent taste, worthy of its important position among the monumental Roman public buildings.

Compared with modern bridges, the piers seem thick, but they were so constructed that they would form abutments for the separate arches, permitting the building of one arch at a time. The difficulty of constructing the foundations below water with the equipment then available may have also influenced their size. This custom of making the piers thick enough to support the unbalanced pressure of an arch on one side persisted through the Roman, Medieval, and Renaissance periods; and it was not until the latter part of the eighteenth century that the engineers designing bridges developed a scientific theory of design, purposely reducing the thickness of the piers so as to take advantage of the balanced thrust from adjacent arches on each side. In the case of the fortified medieval bridge, it was important to have the piers so thick and massive that the destruction of one arch would not cause the piers to be pushed over by the remaining arches, resulting in the collapse of the entire bridge.

The Pons Fabricus or Quatro-Capi in Rome, constructed or repaired by Fabricus about 62 B.C., is similar in arrangement, but simpler than the Pons Palatinus in detail (Plates 34, 35 and 36). It consisted of two arches of about eighty-foot span with a smaller relief arch of about twenty feet over the pier to furnish additional waterway during times of flood. This bridge is of particular interest because it is the first bridge in which the arches do not appear as semi-circular, or "full-centered," as that form is termed. This appears strange because all other Roman arches are full-centered, and it may be that the semi-circle is completed below the water line, the segmental appearance being produced by the submergence of the haunches.

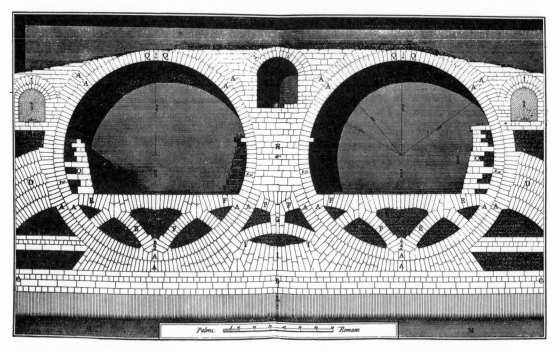

PLATE 36. Section through the Pons Fabricus Drawn by Piranesi. Reproduced from "Roman Architecture, Sculpture and Ornament from Piranesi's Monumental Work," by William Young.

PLATE 37. The Pons Augustus at Rimini. Built about 20 B.C.

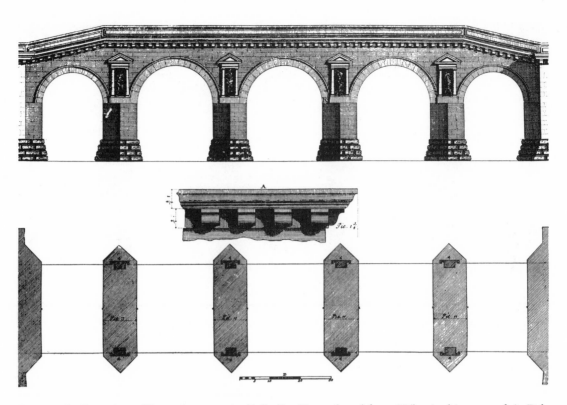

PLATE 38. Drawing of Pons Augustus by Palladio. Reproduced from "The Architecture of A. Palladio," by Giacomo Leoni.

Piranesi's* drawing (Plate 36) shows a very remarkable construction but his authority for this drawing is not known. He shows it as founded on inverted arches below the river bed, the submerged arches joining with the arches of the superstructure to form complete circles. This deep foundation would be so difficult and unnecessary, that it is no doubt a product of Piranesi's fertile imagination, although it is not impossible that shallower inverted arches may have been used.

It was the Pons Augustus at Rimini, with five semi-circular arches of white Istrian stone, built about 20 B.C., that Palladio particularly admired and often copied (Plate 37). It was certainly one of the most beautiful of the Roman works. Above the piers, on the spandrel walls are niches framed with pilasters carrying an entablature and pediment. Over a beautiful cornice supported by modillions is a plain coping rounded at the top. The coping over the center span is higher and on it is engraved an inscription commemorating the construction of the bridge. Less ornate than the Pons Palatinus, the Pons Augustus has a very delicate and

* Piranesi was an Italian architect and etcher of the eighteenth century who made a great many etchings of the architectural antiquities of Rome.

PLATE 39. The Pons Aelius, Rome. Erected by Aelius Hadrianus about A.D. 138

charming character. The motive over the piers has been copied in important bridges in London and Paris.

Palladio said of the Pons Augustus, "But seeing of all the bridges that I have observed, that appears to me to be the finest and the most worthy of consideration (as well as for the strength as the compartment of it) which was built at Ariminum, a city of the Flaminian Tribe, and as I believe by Augustus Caesar. I have given the draughts of it, which are those that follow" (Plate 38). Palladio's drawing does not entirely agree with the photograph, but it shows the origin of the "Palladian Bridge" of the Renaissance.

The Pons Aelius was also one of those which Palladio reported to be almost intact at the middle of the sixteenth century (Plate 39). It was erected by Aelius Hadrianus about 138 A.D., to give access to his own tomb. The foundations were laid with exceptional care with large blocks of dressed stone anchored together in all directions by stone keys and metal clamps. So well was it built that it is still in good condition. Palladio wrote that the Pons Aelius "was anciently all covered with galleries, having columns of brass with statues and other admirable ornaments." The statues of St. Peter and St. Paul at the end of the bridge were erected by Pope Clement VII and the present iron balustrade with the ten statues of angels above the piers was designed by Giovanni Bernini by the order of Pope Clement IX about 1668. The statues,

PLATE 40. The Pons Cestius or Ponte di S. Bartolommeo, Rome

PLATE 41. Ruins of Bridge at Narni, Italy. Built by Augustus Caesar

facing the narrow roadway, high above the lamp poles, do much to injure the scale of a bridge which is otherwise very impressive.

In design, the Pons Aelius differs considerably from the Pons Palatinus and the Pons Augustus. It is more severe and massive. The spandrel walls are plain above the skillfully moulded arch ring or archivolt. The cut-waters at the ends of the piers project out at a sharp angle and above them are strong square pillars which take the place of the niches of the Pons Palatinus. The arches are semi-circular as usual.*

At Narni is one of the largest Roman bridges outside of the city of Rome, constructed by Augustus Caesar to carry the Flaminian Way across the Nera (Plate 41). It was built of white marble with four spans of different widths and heights, the roadway being inclined

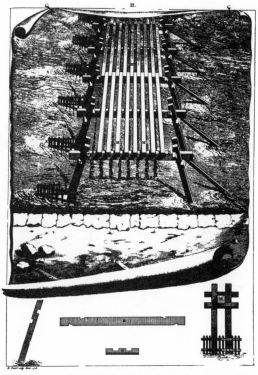

PLATE 42. Palladio's Drawing of a Wooden Bridge Described by Caesar. Reproduced from "The Architecture of A. Palladio," by Giacomo Leoni.

sharply from one bank to the other. Choisy, in his "Art de batir chez les Romains," gives a sketch of the bridge showing the largest span to be 111 feet,† which is greater than any other arch of the Romans. The ruins of this bridge as it stands (according to Degrand, 105 feet high) above the road from Ancone to Rome are extremely picturesque and impressive. In comparing it with other Roman work, Degrand says: "Its ruins are without doubt very beautiful and one sees, in examining the masonry, that the stones were cut and fitted with particular care; but the heaviness of the piers, the inequality of thickness which they present, and which nothing justifies, the different heights of the imposts receiving the haunches of the arches and the absence of all ornamentation permit one to suppose that the appearance of the construction, when new, must have been quite mediocre."

The military strength of the Romans was dependent on their transportation system, a network of excellent highways extending to far distant parts of the Empire. Along these roads

* Degrand in his "Ponts en Maçonnerie" gives the length of the main spans as 60 feet and the thickness of the piers as about 24 feet.
† Sparrow gives the span as 142 feet. "A Book of Bridges," by Frank Brangwyn and W. S. Sparrow.

PHOTO FROM "GRANDES VOÛTES" BY PAUL SÉJOURNÉ

PLATE 43. Roman Bridge over the Touloubre at Saint-Chamas, Bouches-du-Rhone, France, called Pont Flavien.

PHOTO BY LEVY & NEURDEIN

PLATE 44. The Pont du Gard, a Roman Aqueduct near Nîmes, France

were built many bridges, the finest examples of which, outside of Italy, are found in France and Spain. Most of these bridges belong to one of three types, that of the Pons Palatinus, the Pons Augustus at Rimini, or the Pons Aelius. Some of the exceptions will be described later. Degrand points out that the Roman bridges were not always masterpieces. "It has happened, in their time as well as in all other epochs, that either on account of the haste with which certain works were executed, or through lack of money, or because of the incompetence of the architects, some of the bridges were very mediocre works of art devoid of all interest. Their numerous timber bridges and those masonry bridges insecurely built have, of course, not survived." In their military campaigns they needed many temporary timber bridges. Palladio's conception of the wooden bridge described by Caesar is shown in Plate 42, which is reproduced from Palladio's book on Architecture. The description is not complete and the actual details are uncertain.

In France, bridges built by the Romans still span the Vidourle at Sommieres in the Department du Gard, the Coulon near Apt in the Department de Vaucluse, and the Touloubre at Saint-Chamas in the Bouches-du-Rhone. The latter is a particularly beautiful example (Plate 43). It is unusual because at each end it has triumphal arches in an almost perfect state of preservation.

France also possesses the finest of all the Roman aqueducts, the majestic Pont du Gard, built shortly before the Birth of Christ to carry to Nîmes the waters of the fountains of Eure and Airan (Plates 44 and 45). Unlike most of the earlier aqueducts which were single rows of arches, the Pont du Gard consists of three arcades placed one above another. The spans of the two lower arcades are unusually large for works of this kind, being from sixty-five to eighty feet, the larger arches spanning the channel of the River Gardon. There are six arches in the lower arcade, eleven in the center arcade, and thirty-five in the upper. The total height from the river to the water conduit is 155 feet.

As was often done at that time, the stones were dressed with the greatest care and laid up without mortar. The large arches consisted of separate rings side by side with no interlocking of the arch stones; four rings to the lower arches, three to each arch of the middle arcade, and a single ring to the upper arches. This method of constructing arches in unbonded rings is seen in many but not all of the Roman bridges and was copied in some medieval work. Its purpose may have been to permit the construction of the arches one ring at a time, each ring becoming self-supporting when completed, relieving the falsework of the necessity of carrying the weight of the entire arch. Also when no mortar was used, the interlocking of the arch rings would have greatly increased the difficulty of dressing the stone because the face of one

PLATE 45. The Pont du Gard near Nîmes, France

stone would then bear on two others. Only the water conduit of the aqueduct was laid up with small stones set in mortar. The conduit was lined with cement to prevent leakage.

About 400 years after it was built, the aqueduct was broken at each end by barbarians who laid siege to the city of Nîmes and cut off its water supply. Since that time, it has not been kept in repair. At the end of the seventeenth century, during the religious wars, a roadway was corbelled out from the piers along the upstream side of the lower arcade. The passage of cavalry and heavy artillery over this roadway shook the bridge and threw the masonry out of line, developing a curve in the upper arcade. The Providence of Languedoc intervened and restoration was begun in 1670. In 1747, a new highway bridge was completed alongside the arches of the lower arcade. The arches of this new bridge are seen on the far side of the aqueduct in Plate 44.

The stone of the Pont du Gard is a warm yellow limestone. Degrand says: "The character of beauty which the constructors have succeeded in giving to their work is due especially to the great proportions of the monument, its exceptional height, the crudeness, even, of its form in perfect harmony with the abrupt and denuded slopes of the valley it crosses; and in its present state, it should be said, the effect is also the result of the picturesque contours which the ruins present, of the superb and warm color with which time and the mid-day sun have clothed all the material, and finally to the beautiful luminous sky against which it is profiled."

It is difficult in the present age to comprehend the spirit in which these pagan Romans worked. Their masonry was built with a care and skill which amounted to genius. To dress the faces of the stones of a bridge so that they would fit together accurately without a cushion of mortar was a tremendous task. The cost of dressing the stones so precisely would be prohibitive today. An uneven bearing under the load of a high pier or the thrust of an arch would mean a broken stone; but the Romans preferred to take no chance with the crumbling of mortar and their experience no doubt taught them other reasons for not using it. Time has since proved their wisdom.

An arch ring in which the stones were fitted together without mortar was ready to bear its burden as soon as the last stone was set. It was not necessary to wait for weeks until the mortar should gain its strength. Also, the mortarless arch would not settle appreciably when the support of the falsework was removed, and it would not continue to deflect as the mortar shrunk in hardening. Because of the shrinkage and compression of the mortar between the stones, the crown of a large arch will sink several inches from the position in which it is built. The mortar may not be as strong as the solid stone and it introduces an element of weakness.

At Segovia, in Spain, is another magnificent Roman aqueduct of masonry showing their

PLATE 46. The Roman Aqueduct at Segovia, Spain

customary technic (Plates 46 and 47). It is a double arcade 100 feet high, now soaring above the tops of modern houses. The stones of the piers are large, about two feet by four by two in thickness, placed in regular courses. The face of each stone is bordered with a smooth draft cut about an inch and a half wide, with the remainder of the surface roughened with a pick. Some of the arches of this aqueduct were destroyed by wars in the fifteenth century, and Isabella the Catholic had them rebuilt as carefully as possible. In less than three hundred years, the new work had to be repaired while the Roman work was still good. In 1808, Marshal Ney, greatly impressed by the difference between the Roman masonry and the restorations, pointing to the first reconstructed arch, exclaimed, "There begins the work of man!"* It is small wonder that the natives of Segovia believe the legend which attributes the construction of the aqueduct to the Evil Spirit.

Not all of the Roman aqueducts were built of stone. Those arches of the Claudian aqueduct built under the reign of Nero (arcs neroniens A.D. 70) were of brick, their proportions being much lighter and more graceful than those of the stone arches of the same aqueduct built about twenty years earlier. The Alexandrian aqueduct was built of concrete faced with brick.

Spain possesses more fine bridges built during the Roman occupation than any other of the

* From "A Book of Bridges," by Frank Brangwyn and W. S. Sparrow.

PLATE 47. Detail of the Roman Aqueduct at Segovia, Spain

PLATE 48. The Puente Trajan at Alcantara, Spain. Built by Julius Caius Lacer about 98 A.D. at the order of Trajan.

PLATE 49. The Puente Trajan at Alcantara from the bank of the Tagus

[74]

provinces of the Empire. The long life of these structures is explained, at least in part, by the durability of the native stone used in their construction, the favorable climatic conditions, and the fact that the ravages of barbarians rarely extended into Spain. There is, however, no other part of the Roman Empire where the flood waters dash themselves so furiously against masonry placed in their path, and the fortitude of the bridges which have withstood their onslaught for centuries speaks most eloquently of the skill of the Roman engineers. It is said, for instance, of the Puente Trajan, crossing the River Tagus at Alcantara, that the middle piers are 200 feet high, and flood waters have been known to reach the soffits of the arches one hundred and forty feet above the ordinary water level (Plates 48, 49 and 50). And the granite blocks are laid without mortar!

This Puente Trajan was built by the order of Trajan in A.D. 98 by Caius Julius Lacer whose tomb is on the left bank of the river near the bridge. Degrand gives the span of the six arches as from about ninety-two to ninety-eight feet and the thickness of the piers as 29½ feet. He also gives the height of the bridge as about 130 feet. As in the case of other bridges, the dimensions given by different writers do not agree, but the absolute dimensions are not important. This bridge is tremendous, but so perfectly in scale with the great rugged valley in which it is located, that its size is difficult to grasp. The decoration is simple. Its beauty is largely due to the massing of the skillfully executed masonry and the solid dignity of the design which contrasts strong straight lines with the perfect semi-circular arches. The pier ends are square down-stream and pointed up-stream to break the force of the water. They extend up to the springing of the arches, and above them rise strong pilasters which buttress the spandrel walls. The cornice is a simple moulding carried around the tops of the pilasters at the piers. The arch rings are flush with the spandrel walls. Over the central pier is an archway, perhaps trivial for such an imposing bridge but nicely designed nevertheless, bearing the inscription, "Pontem perpetui mansurum in saecula."

The Puente Trajan* has suffered more from warring armies than from the action of the elements. Two of the smaller arches have been destroyed and rebuilt. The Moors first destroyed the smallest arch on the left side of the river in 1214 and it was rebuilt in 1543 with stone from the original quarries twenty-five miles away. Later, the second arch on the right hand side was destroyed by the Spanish to prevent the passage of the Portuguese army. This was repaired by Charles III in 1762 and dynamited in 1809 by the allies of the Spanish to halt the French invaders. It was crossed by Wellington on a suspended roadway of ships' cables covered with planks. Temporary repairs were made in 1819 with wood, and the present

* Arthur Byne's "The Bridges of Spain." *The Architectural Record*, Vol. XL, page 437.

PLATE 50. Detail of the Puente Trajan at Alcantara, Spain

PLATE 51. The Roman Bridge over the Guadiana at Merida, Spain. Down-stream side

PLATE 52. The Roman Bridge at Merida, Spain, from the up-stream side

PLATE 53. The Bridge over the Tormes at Salamanca. The fifteen arches next to the city date from the Roman period; the remainder date from a reconstruction in 1677 by Philip V.

PLATE 54. Roman Bridge at Pont S. Martin, Italy

PLATE 55. Roman Bridge at Lanark

stone arch was built in 1860. The joints of this arch are filled with mortar according to the modern custom.

The low, many-arched bridge over the Guadiana River at Merida, Spain, belongs to a class of Roman bridge distinct from that at Alcantara (Plates 51 and 52). It may have been built under Augustus or Trajan; authorities differ. There are sixty-four arches with a total length of over half a mile, thirty-three feet high and twenty-one feet wide. The piers are rounded at the up-stream end and square down-stream, with small relief arches above. Remnants of a moulded cornice are seen below the parapet. This bridge must also have suffered from warfare, for it was restored in 686 by the Visigoths under Sala and strengthened by Philip III in 1610. During the siege of Badajoz in 1812, seventeen arches were wrecked to halt the enemy.

Many more bridges of the Romans have survived the centuries, but those described will give an idea of their style. The precise workmanship of the best Roman bridges required a discipline and morale among the workmen which could exist only under perfect conditions. The stone masons must have had as thorough training and as high ideals as the engineers who directed the work. Such permanent structures resulted from faith in the permanence of the Roman Empire, and when this faith was shaken there came a change. If Roman statesmen had built as well as Roman engineers, the history of the world would have been different.

From the end of the second century after the Birth of Christ, the quality of their work began to be affected by military anarchy and the invasions of barbarians. Following the establishment of the Empire of the Orient in A.D. 395, no new bridges were built which were comparable to the earlier work.

PART I · SECTION III

THE DARK AGES

THE DARK AGES

WHEN the flame of Roman genius burned out, the art of bridge building was plunged into darkness which lasted for centuries. Even the Empire of the Orient, which remained during the greater part of its existence the most powerful and civilized state of the early Middle Ages, left behind it few bridges and none of great value. This neglect of bridge building prevailed in all countries; nothing of much importance was accomplished until the time of the Crusades.

The same was true of building construction in Western Europe. For several centuries after the fall of Rome, the Celtic and Germanic races were being gradually Christianized. It was not until the eleventh and twelfth centuries that the Romanesque and Norman styles of architecture fully developed. During the latter part of the twelfth century the first Gothic buildings appeared with their pointed arches and vaults. The Gothic style prevailed generally through the thirteenth, fourteenth, and fifteenth centuries, gradually becoming more ornate and elaborate, and finally giving way to the Transitional and Renaissance styles originating in Italy. The Medieval Period of bridge building discussed in this chapter extended from the time of the Romans through the fourteenth century. Strangely, it appears that there were no important permanent bridges erected during the fifteenth century although many beautiful civic buildings and palaces were then built.

From the time when barbarism supplanted Roman civilization, a warlike spirit possessed the world and for centuries little time was devoted to any occupation other than combat. Works of art were not created, but many of those which the Romans had erected in great numbers throughout the Empire were destroyed. This destruction was not immediate and general, and some countries were relatively spared. There were periods of peace and sometimes even attempts at reconstruction, but these could not last long amid the struggles which agitated all peoples. The necessities of war destroyed bridges which time would have spared.

That some consideration was given to bridges during the Dark Ages is proved by instructions addressed by Charlemagne to his Missi-Dominicis, asking them to cooperate in each city with the Bishop and the Count in order to assure the maintenance of public roads and bridges. Also, an order of Louis le Debonnaire in 823 gave an extension of time for the repair of all bridges, and one in 830 ordered the construction of twelve bridges over the Seine. But the

PLATE 56. Jesmond Dene

attempts of Charlemagne to introduce into France institutions similar to those of the Roman Empire were almost without effect. After his death, there were divisions, internal wars, and the separation of all territories into small parts, social conditions preventing the accomplishment of anything useful or progressive. The feudal rulers failed to build new bridges and were unwilling to rebuild old ones when very necessary.

All rivers, even small streams, served as boundaries between the numerous seigneuries. Usually these streams were maintained as naturally fortified frontiers and the establishment of any works which might make the passage easier were vigorously opposed. Warfare was carried on from one bank to the other. The financial condition of these tiny states also prohibited the construction of large bridges.

The splendid ecclesiastical monuments erected under the direction of the clergy or of religious communities as the influence of Christianity spread, prove that the failure to build bridges was not due to the lack of capable architects and skilled workmen. The work of the Romans furnished excellent models, and the difficulties of building foundations in most locations were not insurmountable.

The general system of highways was so defective that improvements were necessary as the relations of nearby states developed and transactions became more important and frequent. Corporations of boatmen were organized and ferries were established across some rivers, but they were often transformed into associations of bandits exacting exorbitant tolls, even robbing and murdering travelers.

Bands of devout men, under the name of congregations of Frères du Pont or Frères Pontifes, undertook to reconcile the various powers whose consent was necessary to establish ferries or build bridges, and to then combine the necessary resources to execute such works. At the same time, these corporations established hospices on the banks of the rivers to shelter and care for poor or sick travelers. From that, they were called "Congrégations Hospitalières."

Degrand says that after the end of the Roman rule, almost seven centuries passed before the first important medieval bridge was built, toward the end of the twelfth century. The dates of some of the early constructions are very uncertain and he has based his deductions on the assumption that no pointed arches were built in the West before the Crusades. That may or may not be true as will be explained later.

Perhaps no other medieval bridge is as famous as the Old London Bridge, started in 1176 by Peter of Colechurch, the chaplain of St. Mary's, and completed thirty-three years later (Plate 58). Before that time, the Thames had been spanned by a timber bridge several times destroyed by flood and fire. With many people living in the houses on the bridge these disasters became so serious that the stone bridge was badly needed. It was an irregular and

PHOTO BY JUDGES, LTD.

PLATE 57. The Auld Brig O'Ayr, Scotland, of the Thirteenth Century.

unsightly mass of masonry with short arch spans and large piers damming up the river so that the water roared through the narrow openings. With the overhanging buildings extending along both sides of the roadway, the chapel on the center pier and the draw-bridge, it was exceedingly picturesque. Until the middle of the eighteenth century, it was the only bridge across the Thames in London. After more than six hundred years of service, it was replaced with a new bridge in 1824.

PLATE 58. The Old London Bridge, from a painting by Monroe S. Orr. Reproduced from *The Builder*, London.

PLATE 59. The Old Pont d'Avignon. Built by Saint Bénézet, 1178–88

Two years after the Old London Bridge was started a very large construction was undertaken in France. A medieval legend* related that a young shepherd named Petit-Benoit came to Avignon in southern France and, inspired from heaven, became in 1178 the instigator and the architect of the bridge which crosses the Rhone at the height of the Rocher des Doms (Plates 59 and 60). This bridge crossed a deep and rapid river about a half mile wide, subject to floods so violent that it seemed nothing could resist them. The means available at that time for founding the piers at such a place, raising the masonry, placing the falsework, and building the arches were so limited that the task must have seemed almost impossible. It can well be understood how such an enterprise struck the imagination of the people who witnessed it and impressed them as a miraculous feat. Benoit, later canonized under the name of Saint Bénézet, had constructed a bridge over the Durance, the Pont du Maupas, in 1164 before going to Avignon to act as head of the Corporation Hospitalière. He was undoubtedly familiar with the Pont du Gard which is not many miles from Avignon.

The work started in 1178 and was finished in ten years in spite of all obstacles. The Rhone opposite Avignon is separated into two branches by an island. Two bridges were constructed separately, one of eight spans and one of five, crossing the branches about perpendicular to the

* According to Viollet-le-Duc, "Dictionnaire Raisonné de l'Architecture Française," 1864.

current. Then across the island, eight more spans were built to fill in the gap. The twenty-one arches had slightly unequal spans, the greatest being over 108 feet. The thickness of the piers was about one-quarter of the length of the span. The piers were about one hundred feet long, so long, in fact, that there was room to build a chapel on the end of one of them. The total width of the bridge was only about sixteen feet and opposite the chapel it was reduced to about six and a half feet, including the parapets, so that it was only suitable for the passage of pedestrians or horsemen and beasts of burden. An enormous undertaking for a footbridge!

St. Bénézet's arches were constructed of four separate rings of stones like the lower arches of the Pont du Gard but the shape of their curve was original. They were in the form of a segment of the end of an ellipse with the small radius of curvature at the center of the span.

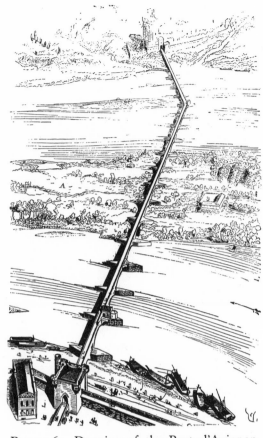

PLATE 60. Drawing of the Pont d'Avignon. Reproduced from Viollet-le-Duc's "Dictionnaire Raisonné de l'Architecture."

What suggested such a curve to him is not known, but it is actually more stable than the circular or the flat elliptical curves commonly used. It may be that he made experiments which showed that arches of that form would stand alone better than circular arches. The arch rings were of uniform thickness for the entire span. The spandrel walls extended up to the top of the parapets without any moulding to mark the roadway. The arrangement of relief arches above the piers as well as the separate rings of the main arches show that St. Bénézet had studied the Roman work.

St. Bénézet died in 1183, five years before the completion of the bridge. It still existed intact in 1385, when Pope Boniface IX, who resided at Avignon, ordered some of the arches demolished to protect himself from the attacks of the inhabitants of the opposite bank of the river. At the time of the construction of the bridge, the jurisdiction of the city extended to both banks of the Rhone, continuing thus until 1307. Then Philippe-le-Bel, having ceded to the Pope his rights to suzerainty over Avignon, contested their validity in so far as the right bank of the river was concerned. In order to affirm his pretentions, he laid the foundations of the formidable defensive tower of Villeneuve which completely commanded the bridge. The popes, on their side, then hastened to erect a fortified chatelet on the left bank. After Pope Boniface IX had cut the bridge to protect himself from the troops occupying the tower of Villeneuve, the demolished arches were repaired by Clément VI. In 1395, the Aragonais and the Catalans cut the bridge during a siege of the palace of the popes and it was not until 1418 that it was repaired by the Avignonnais. Either this last restoration was poorly done or the original work was poor, for in 1602 an arch collapsed carrying with it three others in its fall. Then in 1633, two more arches fell; and finally in the winter of 1670, an exceptional ice flow carried away all but the four arches now standing.

The history of the Pont d'Avignon is typical of most of the bridges built in France during the Middle Ages. The Congrégations Hospitalières of the Frères Pontifes were able to triumph over the difficulties which had prevented the construction of bridges, and they even obtained charters conferring on them certain privileges such as the right to oppose all works of fortification on the bridges or at their approaches and the rights to collect toll. But in spite of these concessions, which they were powerless to enforce, the bridges had scarcely been completed when the people on each bank hastened to protect themselves against their neighbors. Towers, chatelets, and fortresses were built, and became, even in times of peace, the terror of travelers obliged to pass them.

In principle, the seigneurs, who succeeded the Congrégations Hospitalières to collect the tolls for their own profit were not only obliged to keep the bridges in repair, but to guarantee to the travelers the safety of their persons and their belongings, indemnifying the victim or his heirs in case of robbery or murder. Warrants were issued for this purpose against the sire de Crevecoeur in 1254, the seigneur de Vicilon in 1269 and even against the king of France in 1295. But in fact, the corps de garde placed on the bridges usually only annoyed the travelers, exacting tolls even after the bridges were destroyed. The difficulties of obtaining justice were so great that it was better not to attempt it.

The bridge at Saint Esprit over the Rhone is one of the greatest and most imposing of the medieval bridges. Its construction was started in 1265 and completed thirty-two years later. Nineteen of its twenty-five arches have a span of about 78 to 108 feet and its total length is nearly 3300 feet. Viollet-le-Duc says that the Pont Saint Esprit was the last bridge built by the Frères Hospitalières Pontifes. After the thirteenth century, the lay schools of maîtres des oeuvres replaced the religious corporations in both civil and religious constructions; and the cities and seigneurs no more depended on the Frères Constructeurs.

PLATE 61. The Pont de Valentré at Cahors, France. Built in the Fourteenth Century

The Pont de Valentré or the Pont de la Calendre joining the walls of the city of Cahors, France, with the limestone hills across the river, is one of the finest and most complete of the bridges of the fourteenth century* (Plates 61, 62 and 63). It is particularly interesting on account of its strong fortifications, three tall towers, one on the center pier and one at each end, through the gates of which it is necessary to pass in crossing the bridge. The tops of the piers themselves are also crenated to protect the defenders of the bridge from attacks from boats in the river. It is considered the finest of the fortified medieval bridges on account of the completeness of its military works and the regularity and grace of its Gothic design. It has the aspect of a well disciplined warrior.

There are six pointed arches of fifty-four-foot span placed high above the river. Just below the haunch of each arch is a row of holes in which timbers were inserted during construction to support the working platform and falsework for the arches; through the pointed ends of the piers are openings for the passage of men and materials from one platform to another.

The piers of the medieval bridges were of three types. One form, of which the bridge at Avignon is an example, borrowed the relief arch from the Romans. Those at Cahors belonged

* Viollet-le-Duc gives the date of construction as 1251, apparently confusing it with the Pont-Neuf at Cahors, which was built from 1251 to 1283. The Pont de Valentré was built some time during the latter half of the fourteenth century and was the last of three similar bridges of which it is the only one to survive.

PLATE 62. The Pont de Valentré at Cahors, France

PHOTO BY DELL & WAINWRIGHT

PLATE 63. The Pont de Valentré at Cahors, France

to a second type with the ends extending upward to the roadway level forming refuge bays to permit the passing of people and even of carts. This permitted the use of narrow arches. The third type is capped above the springing of the arches with triangular pyramids as in the case of the Pont de la Guillotière at Lyon, France (Plate 64).

The history of the Pont de la Guillotière is uncertain. It is said that the wooden structure preceding the stone bridge was broken down in 1190 under the weight of the baggage train following the armies of Philippe-August and Richard Coeur-de-Lion leaving for the Crusades. The construction of the stone bridge continued for almost four centuries, the work being destroyed by each high flood so that it was not completed until 1570. It originally had a length of about 2130 feet, with twenty arches, nine of which were over the river. About 1840 the bridge was widened to accommodate the increasing traffic. The difficulties encountered in building the bridge are reflected in the shape of the piers. These were made unusually long and sharp to cut the flood waters with as little resistance as possible, and to buttress the spandrels against the pressure. It is interesting to note that this bridge and the bridge at Avignon have piers sharply pointed both up-stream and down-stream, a marked improvement over the Roman method of pointing the up-stream end only. The water converging abruptly below a square pier end forms eddy currents which may loosen the stones or undermine the pier.

Arches in the form of circular arcs or semicircles were used all through the Middle Ages, even when pointed arches were being used exclusively for churches and civic buildings.* The architecture of bridges during that period was not closely associated with that of buildings. The traditional heavy bridge forms were used even after the light and graceful Gothic buildings became common, but the bridges were so designed that they harmonized perfectly with the buildings.

Originating in the East and copied in the West, high pointed or ogival arches were used for bridges only during the medieval period. The general belief is that they were introduced into France about A.D. 1100 by the returning crusaders who had become familiar with them in the Orient, especially at Antioch where Persian works were numerous. It seems true that pointed arches were introduced into the national architecture of France about that time but the theory that none were built in the West previous to the Crusades has been heatedly sup-

* The bridge at Ceret over the Tech River, built in 1336, had a semi-circular arch about 147-foot span, and the bridge at Villeneuve-d'Agen of the fifteenth century a semi-circular arch of 115-foot span. At the end of the medieval period, in 1454, the bridge at Vieille-Brioude was built in the form of a circular arc of 177-foot span, the longest span of any masonry arch built in France before the time of Degrand's writing in 1888. This bridge collapsed after 400 years of service, having been so carelessly built that it is remarkable it stood so long. A much longer span was built at Trezzo over the Adda River in Italy in the fourteenth century, but it was destroyed in 1416 during a local war. The arch was a circular arc of 237-foot span with a radius of about 138 feet. This was 17 feet longer than the Cabin John arch in Washington, D. C., the longest stone span in the world from 1862 to 1903, when the Luxembourg arch was completed.

PHOTO BY LEVY & NEURDEIN

PLATE 64. The Pont de la Guillotière at Lyon, France. Medieval Bridge. Widened about 1840

PHOTO BY KEYSTONE VIEW CO.

PLATE 65. Twelfth Century Bridge at Carcassonne, France. Eleven semi-circular arches of from 36 to 46-foot span.

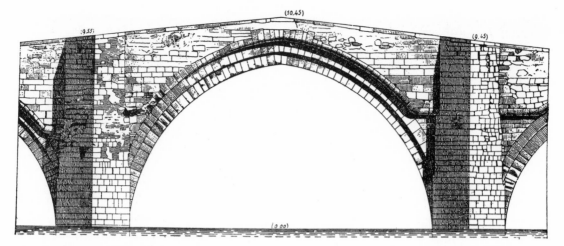

PLATE 66. The Old Bridge at Espalion, France, over the Lot River. Reproduction of Drawing in "Études sur les Ponts en Pierre," by F. de Dartein.

ported and denied by various scholars, there being no definite proof of either contention. The East and the West were more or less in communication at all times and it is very possible that some bridge builder of France may have seen or heard of the pointed arches or may even have made the discovery independently that high pointed arches would exert less pressure against the sides of the piers than the lower semi-circular arches of the Romans.

This controversy has centered especially around the bridge at Espalion over the Lot River in France (Plate 66). In the Province of Rouergue, are several other old bridges quite similar in style to the bridge at Espalion. This bridge has four arches, one almost semi-circular and three slightly pointed, the largest with a span of about fifty feet.*

According to authentic documents, the construction of the Pont d'Espalion was ordered by Charlemagne toward the end of the eighth century. The oldest document which mentions the actual bridge is an old charter of 1050 which is considered by some to be proof that the pointed arches were built before that date. There is, however, nothing to prove that the order of Charlemagne was carried out or that, if a bridge was then built, it was not later reconstructed. As the controversy now stands, each may believe as best pleases him.

The Pont d'Espalion of red sandstone, was originally even more picturesque than it is now. Three fortified towers stood on the bridge, one at each end and one at the center. At one end is a short arch separated from the next span by an unusually thick pier on which one of the towers stood. This small span was replaced with a wooden draw-bridge in 1588 and later

* In the same province, the bridge at Saint-Affrique has one semi-circular arch, apparently rebuilt, and two pointed arches; the bridge at Najac of the thirteenth century has three semi-circular arches, while the Pont Notre-Dame at Entraygues has four pointed arches, of which one is almost round and another is acutely pointed. This latter bridge was in course of construction in 1269.

PLATE 67.   The Thirteenth-Century Bridge at Entraygues, Aveyron, France

PLATE 68. Fortified Bridge at Orthez, France

PLATE 69. Brick and Stone Bridge at Montauban, France. Completed in 1335 by Etienne de Ferrières and Mathieu de Verdun.

rebuilt in 1724. A draw-bridge also existed at the other end of the bridge. The construction of the bridge is unusual and interesting. The ends of the piers and the spandrel walls rise up to the top of the parapets without offset or moulding at the roadway. The arch ring or archivolt is double, the upper ring projecting out beyond the lower. This was a common detail in medieval bridges, but in order to make the roadway still wider, another set of arch stones was placed above the ring, projecting out beyond it to carry the spandrel walls, thereby increasing the distance between the parapets.

The bridge at Albi with seven pointed arches is also of uncertain date. The building of the bridge was decided upon in 1035 and probably started soon after that time but there is no proof of its completion until 1178. At that time the passage of troops over it was mentioned in a document. Degrand calls it a "barbarous work, absolutely without interest," and as such it does not compare favorably with the skillful workmanship of the twelfth and thirteenth centuries.

Another very picturesque French war bridge of the Middle Ages is the bridge at Orthez over the Gave de Pau, with three pointed arches and two high piers springing from the rocky banks in an irregular and interesting manner (Plate 68). The largest span, about forty-nine feet, is nearly twice the length of the others. From the pier at the center, rises a high octagonal tower which was originally duplicated at the other end of the large span. The corbelled parapets along the roadway are the work of the last century. A design of the bridge drawn in lacework, dated 1589, shows the spandrel walls running straight up from the arches and extending some distance above the roadway forming parapets to protect the defenders of the bridge. It is probable that through this parapet above the center of the large span was the opening known as the "Priests' Window." It was through this, after the capture and sack of Orthez in 1560, that the Huguenot soldiers of Queen Jeanne commanded by Montgomery, had cast the Catholic priests taken prisoner. Parts of these parapets were still in place when forty-five riflemen of the rear guard of Marshal Soult, barricaded in the tower of the bridge, held back the English for the entire day of February 27, 1814. The date of the construction of the Pont d'Orthez is not known, but a coin of the City of Orthez dated 1254 bears on one side a picture of one arch of a bridge flanked by two towers. The other two spans were not shown but they probably existed at that time.

The bridge at Montauban over the Tarn, with seven pointed arches of about seventy-foot span, is the most monumental of all the French bridges of the Middle Ages which still stand (Plate 69). It has a length of about 650 feet, with the roadway nearly sixty-five feet above the water. Defensive towers about the size of those of the Pont de Valentré originally stood at each

PLATE 70. The Fourteenth-Century Ponte della Maddalena, sometimes called the "Devil's Bridge," over the Serchio near Lucca, Italy. The arch span is about 120 feet long and 68 feet high.

PLATE 71. Ponte della Maddalena, near Lucca, Italy

PLATE 72. Medieval Bridge at Arenas de San Pedro, Spain

PLATE 73. Medieval Bridge over the River Torto at Camprodón, Spain

end. Except for the limestone coping of the parapets and the quoins of the piers, the bridge is built of red brick, each measuring about 14½ by 9 by 2⅜ inches. Above the piers are arched openings through the bridge probably suggested by the relief arches of the Romans. They are high above the water and their purpose is apparently to save material rather than to relieve flood waters. For the same purpose arched openings were contrived between the spandrel walls above the haunches of the arches. The bridge is skillfully and artistically designed, and well built.

In his argument placing the construction of the first pointed arches in France after the Crusades, Degrand cites the bridge at Montauban as an example of a bridge which was actually built long after its construction was ordered. In the original charter of the City of Montauban, given in 1144, it was provided that the citizens should build a bridge across the Tarn. The city itself had not yet been built at the time and such an undertaking was impossible. Then wars intervened and it was not till 1264 that the consuls of Montauban made financial preparations to build the bridge. Thirty years more passed before it was actually started. The design and construction, carried out by Etienne de Ferrières and Mathieu de Verdun, were completed in 1335, almost two centuries after the charter provided for it.

In spite of their warring, the Italians also found time to build bridges and there are a

PLATE 74. Puente Alcantara over the Tagus at Toledo, Spain, forming part of fortified approach to the city. Built about 1380 by Archbishop Pedro Tenorio. Gateways built or altered about 1480.

PLATE 75. Puente de San Martin over the Tagus at Toledo, Spain, built about 1212 on the site of a Roman bridge destroyed by a flood. Renewed about 1390 by Archbishop Tenorio after the destruction of the large arch. This arch, with a span of 130 feet, is said to be the largest of the old Spanish bridges.

PLATE 76. Medieval Bridge at Besalú, Spain, built on a zig-zag plan to facilitate its defense

PLATE 77. Medieval Bridge on Roman foundations spanning the River Cardoner at Manresa, Spain

PLATE 78. Puente de Piedra and Cathedral at Zaragosa, Spain. 1437

PLATE 79. Bridge of Sixteen Arches over the Guadalquivir at Cordova, Spain, resting on Roman substructure. The Roman arches were destroyed in the eighth century and rebuilt by the Moors in the eleventh century.

PLATE 80. Ponte Castel Vecchio at Verona, Italy. 1355-58

PLATE 81. Ponte Vecchio over the Arno in Florence. 1345

PLATE 82. The Covered Bridge at Pavia, Italy. 1351–56

number of unusually interesting medieval constructions in Verona and Florence and other cities. The Ponte Castel Vecchio over the Adige in Verona was built about 1354 to form a fortified entrance to the city (Plate 80). Degrand states that this is the first known bridge in which the flat elliptical-shaped arch was used; an interesting statement, if true, but unfortunately all three arches are in the form of segments of circles. The span of the large arch is 160 feet, for many years the longest in the world.

The Ponte Vecchio over the Arno in Florence, built in 1345 according to Ferroni, is the first bridge with arches in the form of flat circular arcs of the proportions of modern stone arches (Plate 81). The covered bridge at Pavia has similar segmental arches of somewhat higher rise (1351–56, Plate 82).

Italian war bridges are represented by the Ponte Nomentano (Plate 85) spanning the Arno three miles from Rome, and the thirteenth century bridge across the Nera at Narni (Plate 86). The latter has a tower similar to the French bridge towers. It has suffered considerably, several of the arches having been destroyed and replaced by timber spans as was often the case with medieval bridges because timber spans were easily built, and having been built could more easily be destroyed to prevent the passage of foes.

The Ponte di S. Francesco at Subiaco is an interesting gabled bridge of the fourteenth century (Plate 87). The arch ring, spandrel walls, and parapets are all flush without ornamentation, but the curve of the arch below the sloping lines of the roadway and the gateway tower form a pleasing picture. Curiously, the tower projects over the end of the arch but the appearance is satisfactory because it seems to bring the weight of the tower more directly over the abutment of the arch.

In England, some bridges had been built by the Romans but they were not as impressive either in number or in size as those in France and Spain. The medieval bridges were built largely under the auspices of the church. One of the oldest still standing is the curious triangular bridge of Croyland consisting of three half arches, meeting at the center (Plate 89). It is said to have been built by the Abbot of Croyland about 1380 at the confluence of two streams. In 1854, the streams were diverted and the bridge now stands above dry ground. The sincerity of the abbot in building the bridge has been questioned, as it stood on boggy ground and was so steep that it could not be used by carts or horsemen.

Fortified bridges were built in England as elsewhere. One of these is the bridge gate leading into the fortified town of Monmouth (Plate 90). The arches were ribbed and have been widened since the original construction. On most of the English bridges were chapels, or

PLATE 83. Ponte alla Carraia at Florence. Built in 1218 and destroyed with the Ponte Vecchio in 1333, it was restored in 1337, partly rebuilt by Ammannati and again restored and widened in 1867.

PLATE 84. The Aqueduct at Spoleto, Italy. 266 feet high and 750 feet long, built by Theodelapius, third Duke of Spoleto, in 604. A reconstruction during the fourteenth century is indicated by the pointed arches. The enormous scale of the structure is shown by the size of the buildings.

PLATE 85. The Ponte Nomentano over the Arno near Rome

PLATE 86. Thirteenth-Century War Bridge at Narni, Italy

PLATE 87. Ponte di S. Francesco at Subiaco, Italy. Fourteenth century

PLATE 88. Ponte Pietra at Verona, Italy. A Roman bridge restored in the fifteenth century

shrines of some sort, dedicated to a patron saint. The picturesque chapels were usually erected on a pier near the center of the bridge.

FROM "COUNTRY LIFE," LONDON

The moulding of the archivolt or arch ring in many of the English bridges seems to bear a closer relationship to the forms used in the churches than is noticeable in other countries. It may be that the Roman influence was not as strong in England and many of the bridges were

PHOTO BY JUDGES, LTD.

PLATE 90. Monnow Bridge, Monmouth, England

PHOTO BY JUDGES, LTD.

PLATE 91. The Chantry on Wakefield Bridge

erected by builders of churches who would naturally apply the familiar building forms to the bridges. This similarity is seen at Croyland and Wakefield.

PHOTO BY JUDGES, LTD.

PLATE 92. The Original Front of the Bridge Chantry, Wakefield, England.

The old bridge at Stirling, Scotland, is a fine example of Norman architecture (Plate 94). The piers are massive and nicely proportioned. The semi-circular arch rings are double, the upper ring projecting beyond the lower to gain width for the bridge as at Espalion, France. The spandrel walls rise flush with the upper arch ring up to the top of the parapet without a break. The detail of the coping is interesting, the stones being stepped up, instead of inclined, to follow the slope of the roadway. The entire design is harmonious and dignified. Aside from the double archivolt there is no ornamentation and certainly none is needed.

Degrand classifies the bridges of the Medieval Period into two distinct groups. One is composed of bridges constructed after the manner of the Romans, with modifications due to

PLATE 93. Elvet Bridge, built by Bishop Pudsey in 1170. Later it was widened and the houses erected.

the decadence of the art and the lack of proper equipment. The other group is composed of bridges which particularly characterized the times either on account of their ogival arches, their fortifications, or their picturesque boldness or crudeness of form. Fascinating as these bridges are, their construction was less careful and scientific than that of the Roman bridges. In some cases, the spans of the arches were longer and lighter, but in general they showed less engineering skill in their conception and execution.

Piers were often placed where the ground was most favorable to their founding, the results being irregular spacing, and uneven arch spans. In many cases, it is probable that the design was conceived as the masonry was erected, the arches being merely fitted in between the piers placed in the stream bed at convenient intervals. The piers were constructed one after another, perhaps one or two a year. The foundations were prepared by dumping stones in the river or placing them in baskets until a mound was formed on which the regular masonry of the piers could be laid. These mounds of stone filled up the bed of the stream. The piers were so wide and the spans between them so short that comparatively little waterway was left and flood waters passed with difficulty, sometimes washing away the bridge. The piers of the London bridge so acted as a dam that the water level was considerably higher at the up-stream side of the bridge than at the down-stream side; and the water rushed through with such rapidity that it was difficult for a boat to pass. The massive looking piers were sometimes only shells of stone filled with tamped earth. Some of the Roman piers were faced with stone and filled with concrete and mortar.

The weight of the large, massive piers compacted the foundations so that comparatively slight additional settlement was to be expected when the arches were built. Otherwise the arches would have been distorted and broken. Each span was a unit placed between piers of

PLATE 94. Old Bridge near Stirling, Scotland

sufficient stability to support the unbalanced thrust of the arch on one side, before the next arch was in place. This permitted the construction of the spans one at a time, year after year, and also prevented the collapse of the entire bridge when one of the spans was destroyed. It sometimes happened that the arch stones were worn entirely through at the crown by traffic, and it was necessary to replace them one by one. The clumsy piers therefore served a dual purpose. They compacted the foundations before the arches were placed and they supported each arch independently of its neighbors.

The length of the piers also served a purpose aside from the cutting of flood waters, and the fending off of ice and debris. The ends of the piers were used to support temporary timber

PLATE 95. Bridgend, Berwick-on-Tweed, England.

bridges necessary during construction or repair, and to afford a passage during the long years while the stone bridge was under construction. These timber bridges permitted the collection

PLATE 96. Stopham Bridge, Sussex, England

PLATE 97. Karlsbrücke, Prague. Completed early in the fourteenth century. The sixteen spans, varying from about 55 to 76 feet, were unusually large for that time.

PLATE 98. Wilton Bridge, Ross, England. Ribbed arch with Z-shaped joints

PLATE 99. Kreutznach on the River Nahe in Prussia

[117]

of tolls to assist in paying for the construction; and in some cases tolls were collected even after the stone bridge had been destroyed.

In order to reduce the lateral pressure on the piers, the arches were made as high as possible from springing to crown. The haunch of the arch was placed as low as possible on the pier to reduce the overturning effect. The early ogival, or pointed arch, was higher than the semi-circular arch in proportion to the span, and the lateral thrust against the pier was correspondingly smaller. The use of semi-circular arches or high ogival arches necessitated in many cases a steeply inclined roadway in order to pass over the span, as in the bridge near Lucca. Flat arches which made possible a nearly level roadway and a great saving in masonry were not used until the fourteenth century. One important innovation for which this period must be given credit is the ribbed arch. The Romans had built arches of several ribs placed together as in the Pont du Gard, a detail followed in the Pont d'Avignon, and Pont Saint Esprit. Several medieval bridges were built with the ribs separated and the space between slabbed over with thin stones. Thus a ribbed soffit was formed, as at Monmouth in England, and in the bridge over the Thouet near Airvault in France. The origin of this type of construction is uncertain, but it is worthy of note as a scientific attempt to save material and weight in the arches. The ribbed arch of the Wilton Bridge over the Wye is particularly interesting because the joints between the arch stones are made Z-shaped to prevent the stones from slipping (Plate 98).

In Persia, where stone was lacking, the medieval bridges were usually built of brick with pointed arches. On account of the scarcity of wood for the falsework on which the arch was carried until it became self-supporting, an interesting detail was devised. The lower parts of the arch, the haunches, instead of consisting of an arch ring separated from the masonry above, were bonded in with the piers and built for nearly half of the height of the arch without timber supports. The upper part of the arch was built of several courses, the lower of which were placed on light falsework by child masons. The upper courses were laid on the completed lower courses, so that the entire weight did not come on the timber. The Romans also applied these methods to some stone arches, but did not carry the bonded haunches so high as the Persians.

Perhaps the most striking feature of medieval bridge engineering was the courage and perseverance of the builders. They undertook works of unprecedented size without having at their disposal sufficient funds or proper equipment for doing such difficult work. They struggled for many years with incessant wars interfering and finally succeeded in completing bridges which served their purpose for centuries.

PART I · SECTION IV

THE RENAISSANCE

THE RENAISSANCE

OUT of the strife and oppression of the Dark Ages there was born a profound intellectual movement which resulted finally in establishing the rights of the individual, on which modern civilization is based. The roots of this movement extended back into the Middle Ages, first developing in Italy, where the feudal system was less firmly planted, and then spreading to the other countries of Europe. Under its influence the world gradually became a place in which to live in peace and happiness. The different phases of this Renaissance period lasted from the fifteenth century to the end of the seventeenth. The "rebirth" of art was due to awakened interest in classical studies, and a new appreciation of the beautiful things of life. This joy of living found expression in the development of both art and science, and was reflected in the building of bridges which possessed a new beauty and grace quite modern in feeling.

The pagan Roman art was reborn with a Christian spirit. The Romans had applied the same principles of art in designing both their bridges and their buildings. They had made a studied attempt to design the bridges so that they would be entirely in harmony with their surroundings. Their urban bridges were urbane in character, more formal and refined than those of the military roads in the open country.

During the period which followed the fall of the Roman Empire, there appears to have been little in common between the architectural design of bridges and that of buildings. The traditional forms were followed in bridge building, or were modified to suit the physical conditions. Many of the medieval bridges were undoubtedly built without any complete preconception or detailed design. The piers were founded wherever the bed appeared favorable.

PHOTO BY JUDGES, LTD.

PLATE 100. Henley Bridge on the Thames, England.

PLATE 101. Detail of the Ponte alla Paglia, Venice. Built in 1360 and restored in 1847

PLATE 102. Ponte di San Giobbe, Venice

The bridges were for the most part military works subject to frequent destruction. Comparatively few bridges were built; and with the means available, the construction of a strong permanent bridge was so much of a feat in itself, that little thought was given to decoration. Even during the twelfth and thirteenth centuries when beautiful Gothic cathedrals were being built as a protest against feudalism, the new architectural details were not adopted by bridge builders. There were, of course, some exceptions to this rule as the Gothic bridge at Croyland and some of the bridge towers; but, in general, bridge building appears to have been a separate art.

In the fourteenth century, the bridge at Verona and the Ponte Vecchio at Florence show careful architectural design. Another bridge, the Ponte alla Paglia over the canal in Venice, said to have been built in 1360, is a beautiful design in the Italian Gothic style (Plate 101). These three examples show that bridge design was re-established as an architectural art before the end of the Gothic period.

The more notable bridges of the Renaissance were built in important cities. As urban bridges, they were appropriately decorated with a quiet good taste which permitted them to exist harmoniously among their neighbors. They were neither garish nor shabby, and they attended to their business in a very convincing and dignified manner. They carried the streets on their backs more easily without humping high in the air, as did many medieval bridges, and they wisely withdrew their feet from the streams as much as possible to allow the water to pass peacefully on its way.

The passing of the medieval period of barbaric structures and the renewal of the Roman tradition in bridge building is definitely marked in Italy by the construction of the bridge called the Ponte Corvo, or Curved Bridge, over the torrential River Melza near Aquino. It was commenced in 1502 by Stefano del Piombino who curved the bridge up-stream in order to help the piers oppose the current. There were seven semi-circular spans increasing in size from seventy-four feet six inches at the ends to about ninety-four feet at the center. The piers were only thirteen feet thick, the proportions being much lighter and more graceful than those of previous bridges. The axis of the bridge followed the arc of a circle of about 577-foot radius and the center lines of the piers pointed to the center of the circle. The arches being wider at one side of the bridge than the other, the cutting of the arch stones required special skill; but in spite of the difficulty in building the arches and in placing the foundations, the bridge has stood for more than four centuries without any important reconstruction. The decoration of the bridge was very simple and satisfactory. Before its completion, in 1505, the architect who designed it died, and the work was carried on by Brother Joconde, to whom was given much of the credit for the success of the bridge. He was called to France by Louis XII to direct the

PLATE 103. Bridge Design by Palladio

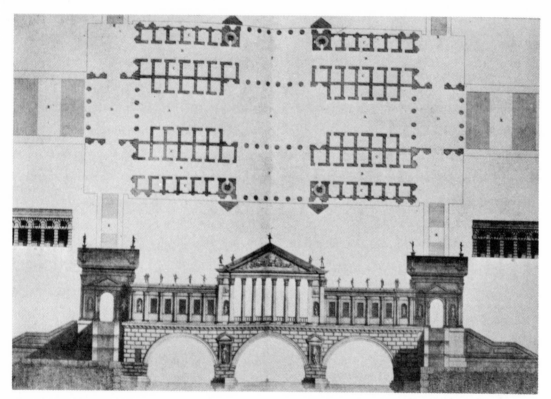

PLATE 104. Palladio's Design for the Rialto Bridge, Venice. Sixteenth century

construction of the Pont Notre-Dame, the first stone bridge of Paris. It was through the campaigns of Charles VIII and Louis XII, who spent several years in Rome, that the Renaissance architecture was introduced into France.

The old Pont Notre-Dame of Paris was started in 1500 and completed in 1507. The foundations of piles surrounded by stones were so well built that they were again used for the new bridge built in 1853. The old bridge had six semi-circular arches of about fifty-one to fifty-six-foot span with piers about sixteen feet thick. The ornamentation was similar to that of the Ponte Corvo. It was the first bridge in which the curve of the archivolt at the face of the spandrel wall was given a larger radius than the barrel of the arch, producing a funnel-like flaring out at the haunches of the arches. This detail, called the corne-de-vache, or cow's horn, was much used in later bridges. This bridge had a width of about seventy-six feet; but unfortunately for its appearance, a double row of houses was built along the roadway, leaving a street only twenty-one feet wide. Three of the spans were completely obstructed below, causing the Seine to rise about sixteen inches at the up-stream side of the bridge.

In Italy, about the middle of the sixteenth century, a number of bridges were built by Palladio, one of the most talented architects of the Renaissance. He adapted the details of the Roman bridges and frequently used the motive of the bridge at Rimini with the ornamental niches over the piers. He made a design for the Rialto Bridge over the Grand Canal in Venice which unfortunately was not carried out (Plate 104). In his own words, "Very fine, in my opinion, is the design of the following bridge, and perfectly suited to the place where it was to be built, which was in the middle of one of the greatest and most celebrated cities of Italy, the metropolis of many other cities and trading almost to all parts of the world. The river is very large, and the bridge was to have been built just at the very spot where the Merchants

PLATE 105. The Rialto Bridge, Venice, by Antonio Da Ponte. 1588–92

PLATE 106. The Bridge of Sighs, Venice

PLATE 107. Bridge at Pontassieve, Italy. 1555

come together to negotiate and treat of their affairs. Wherefore, as well to preserve the grandeur and dignity of the said City, as very considerably to increase the revenue of the same, I designed the bridge so broad as to make three streets upon it; that in the middle large and fine, and the other two on the sides somewhat less." Without the palatial superstructure, the bridge itself is quite simple and dignified. It has details in common with both the Pons Augustus at Rimini, and the Pons Aelius. The treatment of the piers is especially interesting. They are of heavy rusticated stonework, extending up above the springing of the curve of the arches in the manner of the Persian bridges.

Some years after Palladio made his design for the Rialto Bridge, the City of Venice held an open competition which was won by the design of Antonio da Ponte, whose bridge was built in 1590 (Plate 105). It has a single span of nearly ninety-four feet, richly ornamented with moulded archivolt, cornice, balustrade, and carvings on the spandrels. There are two rows of shops with passages along the center and the railings. Although less monumental than Palladio's design, it is considered one of the finest of the Italian bridges.

Of all of the Renaissance bridges, the Ponte S. Trinita over the Arno in Florence is the most remarkable in its grace and originality (Plates 108 and 17). It was built from 1567 to 1570 from the design of Bartolommeo Ammannati who invented a new form for the three arches.

PLATE 108. One Arch of the Ponte S. Trinita, Florence, 1570, with the Ponte Vecchio in the background

PLATE 109. Ponte di Mezzo, Pisa, Italy

They are flat and slightly pointed at the center, the curve being almost straight near the center of the span. The radius of curvature decreases toward the piers until the intrados becomes vertical as it touches the side of the piers. This form has been described as two intersecting ellipses; but it is so delicate that it appears to follow no mathematical rule at all, as though the designer with great skill had drawn free-hand the curve he thought the most beautiful. It flows smoothly from the springing to the center, where the angle between the two intersecting curves is cleverly eased by the introduction of a carved keystone below a cartouche of excellent design. The moulding of the archivolt and the solid parapet harmonize with the curve of the arch.

The length of the side spans is given by Degrand as about eighty-six feet and the center span as about ninety-six, with the pier thickness twenty-six feet. The thickness of the piers has not escaped criticism but it is probable that the designer wished to add to the apparent solidity of the bridge by thickening the piers to compensate for the unusual lightness of the spans. Structurally, the thickness of the piers is justified by the flatness of the arches and the height of the haunches above the bed of the stream. The bridge is not, after all, a modern construction. It was necessary to build the piers strong enough to support the arches independently, and a flat arch would push over a high, slender pier.

The entire design of the Ponte S. Trinita is nicely composed. The roadway is gently curved up over the bridge, the center span being longer and higher than the others. As a final touch, four statues were placed at the entrance to the bridge at the ends of the parapets, and unlike those of the Pons Aelius, these statues are nicely in scale with the bridge.

The form of the Ponte di Mezzo at Pisa, built in 1660, was probably suggested by the Ponte S. Trinita but it lacks the spirit of the older bridge (Plate 109). The three arches are flat circular arcs, with a rise of only one-sixth of the span length. Degrand gives the spans as sixty-eight feet for the side arches and seventy-eight feet for the center. The piers are about twenty feet thick and similar in form to those of the Ponte S. Trinita. The subtle curve of the roadway has been replaced by straight lines. Although less graceful and heavier in appearance than the Florentine bridge, it has a satisfying beauty which is heightened by the use of white marble for the archivolts and moulded courses. It is well designed to fit into the architectural setting formed by the developments along the river banks. The bridges of Florence and Pisa occupy very fortunate positions, in common with those of many other European cities, because they are made conspicuous by open water fronts and have an opportunity to beautify and be beautified by their surroundings.

The Renaissance bridges of France followed the best Roman tradition as did those of Italy.

PLATE 110. Chenonceaux, France, the wing across the Cher erected for Catherine de Medici on arches built for Duchesse Diane de Poitier by Philip de l'Orme in 1556.

[131]

PHOTO FROM "GRANDES VOÛTES" BY PAUL SÉJOURNÉ

PLATE III. The Old Bridge at Toulouse, by Pierre Souffron and Jacques Lemercier. 1542–1632.

The beautiful new designs created during this period form a background for the more scientific bridge building of the eighteenth century. The history of a number of these bridges drawn from old manuscripts is given by de Dartein * in an interesting manner together with carefully prepared scale drawings showing all important details. As well as for their historical interest, these drawings are particularly of value because many of the details are worthy of adaptation in modern work. A beautiful collection of sketches, paintings, and measured drawings is also given in "Old Bridges of France," by William Emerson and Georges Gromort.

The most important of the French Renaissance bridges are the Pont de Pierre over the Garonne River at Toulouse, the Pont Henri IV at Châtellerault, and in Paris, the Pont-Neuf, the Pont Saint-Michel, the Pont Marie, and the Pont Royal. Others were built but the ones named are representative of their architectural style. During that period, many magnificent châteaus were built and most of these had bridges over moats or adjacent streams. The design of these small bridges is interesting because they were decorated in the same style as the buildings which they served. The châteaus of this period were no longer the dark, formidable

* "Études sur les Ponts en Pierre Remarquables par leur Décoration antérieurs au XIXe Siècle," by F. de Dartein. Ch. Béranger, Paris. 4 volumes.

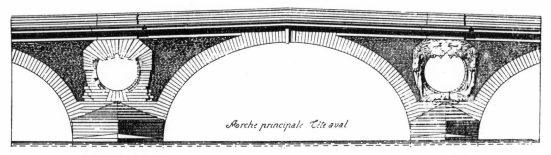

Arche principale Tête aval

PLATE 112. Proposed carving of piers of the Old Bridge at Toulouse. Reproduced from a drawing in "Études sur les Ponts en Pierre," F. de Dartein.

fortresses of the Middle Ages, but beautiful, cheerful buildings whose style is still copied by modern architects.

The largest and in many respects the most unusual of the French Renaissance bridges is the Pont de Pierre over the Garonne at Toulouse, also called the "Pont-Neuf" and "Grand Pont" (Plates 111 and 112). The site of the bridge was selected and the original design was made by a committee of master masons and carpenters from Toulouse, Agen, Montauban, Moissac, and Cahors called together by the Capitouls of Toulouse in 1542. The first stone was placed the following January and the work on the foundations, a continued struggle against physical difficulties and labor troubles, was carried on for more than seventy years. The first arch was not started until 1614. The foundations were built on bed rock inside the excavations, kept dry by cofferdams of two rows of sheet-piles with clay tamped between to make them watertight. According to Vitruvius, this method was also used by the Romans in the Tiber. The piers at Toulouse were built successively, the construction of each being

PLATE 113. Pavilion of the Old Bridge at Toulouse, by Mansart. 1686. Reproduced from a drawing by F. de Dartein.

[133]

accompanied by the religious and civic rites usually celebrated only once for an entire bridge.

During the progress of the work, the arrangement of the piers was entirely changed from the original design. The spans were lengthened and widened, providing more waterway and a longer bridge of monumental proportions in place of the rather insignificant structure of the original concept. A number of masters were successively in charge of the work and it is not known to whom the credit for the change in plan is due. The superstructure was designed by Jacques Lemercier, Architect to the King, who had become dissatisfied with the slow progress and had put his commissioners in charge of the work. It was finally completed in 1632, almost a century after it was commenced.

The Pont de Pierre is unsymmetrical, with seven arches of unequal spans, the largest of which (104 feet) is the third from the right-hand bank. The five arches at this end of the bridge are elliptical, and Degrand says that this is the first appearance of the elliptical arch in the bridges of France, having as precedent only the arches of the bridge at Verona in Italy. Since the latter were actually circular arcs and not elliptical, it may be that the arches of Toulouse were the first of that form in the world.

Another feature which adds greatly to the beauty of this bridge is the use of brickwork in the spandrel walls and the arch soffits, which contrasts pleasingly in color with the cut stone used for the rest of the superstructure. The brickwork of the arch soffits is relieved by five rings of stone equally spaced between the stone arch rings at the spandrels, all bonded in with the brickwork. The cylindrical openings through the bridge above the piers are useful as well as ornamental because they are large enough to increase the waterway appreciably at time of flood. These openings are surrounded by rings of stone which were to have been sculptured to represent the mask and skin of a lion. De Dartein gives a drawing of this detail taken from an engraving by Berthault dated 1783 (Plate 112).

On account of the thickness of the piers, the heaviness of the arches and the irregularity of the entire arrangement, the Pont de Pierre presents an interesting combination of medieval characteristics with the elegance of the Renaissance. In 1686 a beautiful triumphal archway designed by Jules Hardouin Mansart was built at the end of the bridge, away from the city (Plate 113). Unfortunately this left only a narrow roadway so it was removed in 1860 to provide for the increasing traffic.

While he was energetically hastening the construction of the bridge at Toulouse, Henry IV completed the Pont-Neuf at Paris, and the Pont Henri IV at Châtellerault. This latter is somewhat similar in type to that at Toulouse but quite different in design (Plate 114). Its nine spans cross the wide River Vienne and connect Châtellerault with its suburb, Châteauneuf.

PLATE 114. The Pont Henri IV at Châtellerault, by Laurent Joquet and Gaschon Belle. 1576–1611

The width of the bridge was unusually great for one of the smaller cities, being surpassed by only two of the French Renaissance bridges.*

At the Châteauneuf end of the Pont Henri IV was an imposing gateway consisting of two large circular towers connected by a rectangular pavilion (Plate 115). Although this gateway

PLATE 115. Pavilion of the Pont Henri IV at Châtellerault. Reproduced from a drawing by F. de Dartein.

* The widths of the five most important were about as follows: The old Pont Saint-Michel 81 feet, the Pont Marie 77 feet, the Pont Henri IV 71.5 feet, the Pont-Neuf at Paris 66 feet and the Pont de Toulouse 65.5 feet.

from a distance had the military aspect of the medieval fortified bridge towers, it actually was not fortified. It lacked the former crenations, machicolations, and small archers' windows. Apparently its principal purpose was to lend dignity to a monumental bridge. It marked the transition from the medieval fortifications to the ornamental archways of Louis XIII and Louis XIV, such as those at Toulouse and Montauban. It was given some military value by the placing of a moat between the gateway and the shore, crossed by a narrow bridge of two arches and a draw span, or "pont-levis." It is curious that so important a bridge with a width of over seventy feet should be accessible only over a narrow draw-bridge fourteen feet wide. To provide for modern traffic, the approach has been widened and the center part of the gateway between the towers has been removed, resulting, as at Toulouse, in a considerable loss of beauty.

The Pont Henri IV was designed by the architects of Charles IX, Laurent Joguet and Gaschon Belle, who were sent from Paris in 1564, about eight years after the former timber bridge had been carried away by a flood. The work on the foundations was started in 1576 and the bridge was completed about 1611, thirty-five years later. The details of the Pont Henri IV are unusual. The spans were all nearly the same length, about thirty-two feet, with piers fifteen feet thick. The center arch is almost semi-circular and the others are elliptical, increasing in flatness toward the river banks, the crowns being successively lower to accommodate the grade of the roadway. The elliptical appearance of the arches was exaggerated by the flaring corne-de-vache at each side. Since the corne-de-vache appears at both the up-stream and down-stream sides, its purpose must have been to gain width for the bridge without lengthening the piers, rather than simply to facilitate the passage of the flood waters. The same device was used to widen the small arm of the Pont-Neuf, in Paris, after the pier foundations had been built.

Another unusual arrangement is the carrying of the cornice and sidewalk at one level for the full length of the bridge instead of having them follow the grade of the roadway. This may have been done to provide a level emplacement for buildings to be built on the bridge. The buildings, however, were never constructed. This disposition required an increasing height of spandrel wall between the arch and the cornice from the center to the end of the bridge, and an increasingly high curb between the roadway and sidewalk. The prominent cornice with strong projection carried on massive consoles is purely a work of the Renaissance. The details were inspired by the classical doric frieze which were adapted with the characteristic freedom of the Renaissance period. All of the other details of the ornamentation are in excellent accord.

PLATE 116. Pont-Neuf, the Short Arm, by du Cerceau and Marchand. 1578–1607

PLATE 117. The Long Arm of the Pont-Neuf, Paris

PLATE 118. Central Span of the Short Arm of the Pont-Neuf, Paris. Reproduced from a drawing by F. de Dartein.

About four years before the completion of the Pont Henri IV at Châtellerault, the Pont-Neuf at Paris was finished (Plates 116, 117 and 118). Of this romantic and beautiful bridge, volumes have been written. There is no bridge in any country which more deserves the attention it has received. De Dartein's introduction to his monograph on the Pont-Neuf is so colorful that a translation of part of it is given: "The following picture, drawn by M. Hanotaux, gives a good idea of the exuberant and picturesque life swarming incessantly on the bridge.

"Immediately on its completion, the Pont-Neuf became the important thoroughfare between the two banks. From one side as from the other, Paris flocked there. Standing in the shelter of one of the circular balconies bordering the bridge, one beheld the incessant and variegated spectacle of the Parisian crowd, a crowd infinitely less monotonous and orderly than that of today. Something of the tumult of the Ligue still circulated in it.

"The busy activity of the bourgeois, the sprightly sauntering of the idler, the blustering vanity of the cadet à l'espagnole, the insolence of the public women, the haughtiness of the seigneurs of high society, the haste of the courtesans passing toward the Louvre, cavaliers, pedestrians, carriages, sedan chairs, all rolled by in an interminable circulation. The mountebanks, fortune tellers, quack doctors, and tumblers, having established themselves there, attracted thither loafers, thieves, swordsmen, swindlers and pick-pockets.

"There was a proverb that one never crossed the Pont-Neuf without meeting there three things: a monk, a girl and a white horse.

"The roadway of the bridge was quite poorly maintained and had more holes than paving stones. Filth piled up at the foot of the bronze horse.* A crowd of small portable booths pressed on the sidewalks. The great distraction for the Parisian was first the 'Samaritaine,' a hydraulic pump constructed alongside the second pier from the side of the Louvre. Its façade which faced the bridge was richly decorated. The principal motive represented Jesus in conversation with the Samaritan near the well of Jacob. This group, the clock, the chimes which played various tunes, and the Jacquemart which struck the hours, became for two centuries a fertile subject of pleasantries for the Parisian causticity. There were hundreds of political pamphlets which referred to the Samaritaine and the Jacquemart.

"The loiterer could next stop to listen to the merchants of new songs, the recital of poems of the cross-roads or the lotteries or the show of the tooth-pullers who often directed veritable troupes of comedians. All the oral and familiar literature of the times was connected with the Pont-Neuf, from Tabarin to Brioché, from Cormier, a rival of Molière, to Dassoucy, from 'Francion' to the 'Roman Bourgeois.' Good or evil, it was there the heart of popular Paris beat. In this land of laughter, the pun of Tabarin, the song of Pont-Neuf, the pleasantry of Gauthier Garguille, often had a penetrating force and a power of opinion which held in respect the will of the prince and the authority of the law.

"The history of Pont-Neuf, with its events, incidents and anecdotes connected with it, has been agreeably presented, in two small scholarly volumes by M. Edouard Fournier.† There is everything in this history. The dramatic mingles with the comic. Riots, murders and corporal punishments alternate with jests and songs."

One would not be inclined to criticize the architecture of a bridge with such romantic historical associations and fortunately for Paris there is very little cause for criticism. Crossing the two branches of the Seine at the lower end of the Ile de la Cité with the little Parc du Vert Galant below it, framed between the wooded embankments and the city on each side, it is one of the most beautiful sights of Paris. The design is unique. The arches and piers are of sturdy proportions, well in scale with the buildings of the city. Compared with a modern bridge, its many piers seem to obstruct the waterway unnecessarily, but increasing the length of the spans would not help it to fit into the picture more harmoniously. The plain spandrel walls are crowned with a classical cornice supported on grotesquely carved consoles. The end arches are flared out in plan at their junction with the quays to permit convenient access to the bridge.

* The statue of Henri IV on the island.
† "Histoire du Pont-Neuf," by Edouard Fournier. Published without date by Dentu, Paris.

To fully appreciate the bridge itself, it is necessary to know something of the story of its construction. In 1550, Henry II was asked to build a bridge near the Louvre because the growth of the city had overloaded and almost broken down the old Pont Notre-Dame. At that time, it was too much of an undertaking for the city to finance; but when the request was later renewed, Henry III ordered its construction in 1577 at the expense of the national treasury. The king appointed a commission of prominent men to direct the work; and this commission, with the help of a technical board of master masons, carpenters and architects, selected the site and prepared a design. This design, which was fortunately not followed, provided triumphal arches at each end and a large two-story pavilion over the square on the island. There may have been political reasons for the suggestion of these triumphal gateways, because it would have been a simple matter to barricade them in case of an uprising and prevent the king from reaching the parliament. The decoration was greatly inferior to the final design, but it is interesting to note that it did not show houses on the bridge such as the other bridges carried.

In 1578, the commission was given authority to proceed with the construction of the bridge and they advertised for bids for the masonry of the foundations of the piers of the short arm. The contract was to be awarded to the lowest bidder; but because the low bidders were not considered competent, the work was readvertised twice before it was finally awarded. Of the six contractors who started on the foundations, only two, Guillaume Marchand and François Petit remained on the work until the completion of the bridge. During the year 1578, the foundations of the four piers and one abutment of the short arm were completed. The masonry rested on wood platforms on the bed of the river six feet below the water level.

It appears probable that the design of the bridge as built was made by the king's architect, Androuet du Cerceau, in 1579, before the contract for the arches of the short arm was awarded. In 1579, the plan was also changed to provide for houses on the bridge requiring a widening of the roadway. Since the bases of the piers of the short arm were already built, the flaring cornes-de-vache were necessary to permit carrying the widened arches out over the pointed pier ends. The piers of the long arm, built after the change, were themselves lengthened and the cornes-de-vaches were not used. Fortunately the houses were never built, in spite of the preparations.

During the next nine years, the piers of the long arm were built and the arches of the short arm were completed except for the filling of the haunches, a foot walk being built over them. In 1588, religious wars and political disturbances stopped the work on the Pont-Neuf; and it was not resumed until 1599 when Henry IV had pacified the kingdom and made peace with

Spain. The short arm was then completed and the piers of the long arm were repaired where the foundations had been scoured by the current. In 1601, Henry IV ordered that the bridge be completed within three years, and in June, 1603, he undertook a rather hazardous crossing of the still unfinished bridge. Two years later, he crossed for the first time on horseback and it was finally completed in 1607.

The Pont-Neuf, as most of the French bridges of the Renaissance, was built on poor foundations. Toward the end of the eighteenth century, it was also evident that the arches of the long arm had been built too hastily. The list of repair work done on the bridge is a long one. The most important reconstruction was done from 1848 to 1855 when the seven spans of the long arm were rebuilt and the roadway was lowered by changing the arches from an almost semi-circular form to elliptical. The arches of the short arm were repaired without rebuilding and their form is therefore little changed. Over the entire length of the bridge, the sidewalks were lowered and the faces of the piers, spandrels, cornices and carved consoles which had crumbled were rebuilt. Every effort was made to conserve the form and character of the old work. Four sculptors, among whom was Barye, carved the masks of the consoles, reproducing as nearly as possible the original ones and making no two alike.

Again in 1885, one of the piers of the short arm, the second from the left bank, was undermined and destroyed the two adjacent arches. These were rebuilt and all of the foundations were strengthened.

Although authorities differ and absolutely definite information is lacking, the credit for creating this magnificent work of art appears to be due to Baptiste Androuet du Cerceau and to Guillaume Marchand. The engineers who have repaired and restored it also deserve credit for making it permanent. Among these were Soufflot, Perronet, Lagalisserie and Résal.

In addition to the Pont-Neuf, there were three other important Renaissance bridges in Paris, the Pont Marie, Pont Royal, and the former Pont Saint-Michel.

The Pont Marie, extending from the right bank of the Seine to the Ile Saint-Louis, was built on one of the sites considered for the Pont-Neuf (Plate 119). The contract for its construction was unusual. It provided that Christofle Marie and his associates should build the bridge at their own expense, receiving in return the grant of the Ile Notre-Dame and the Ile aux Vaches on which they should build houses. The stream between the two islands was filled later and they became the Ile Saint-Louis. The bridge was designed by Marie or by some unknown artist employed by him. Construction was started in 1614 and completed in 1635.

The Pont Marie and its foundations have been extensively reconstructed because the original work was poorly done. On the night of March 1, 1658, two of the arches and the houses

PLATE 119. Pont Marie, Paris, by Christofle Marie. 1614–35

on them were carried away by a flood. For six years the gap was filled with a wooden bridge, and when the arches were rebuilt the houses were not built over them. The other houses remained on the bridge until 1789, when most of the bridges of Paris were cleared of houses. The roadway was then widened and lowered, flattening the grades, and broad sidewalks were provided. Extensive repairs again became necessary in 1850.

The Pont Marie originally had six arches, one of which was later built into the quay. Of the five remaining arches, the largest span (about 58 feet) is not the center but to the left of the center, and is an elliptical arch, while the others are semi-circular. The piers have sharp triangular cutwaters at both ends with moulded pyramidal caps. Above the piers are framed niches, no doubt suggested by those at Rimini, although they are more ornate in character. Instead of the usual classical cornice of the majority of the French Renaissance bridges, there is only a thin moulded band of considerable projection with a plain parapet above. Aside from the niches, the spandrels are plain. The arch stones are bonded into the stonework of the spandrel walls somewhat as in the case of the Pont-Neuf. The arch stones of the Pont Marie are longer and more irregular, increasing in length toward the crown of the arches. The ornamentation of the bridge is refined and in good scale. The plain masonry and the proportions of piers and arches give the bridge an appearance of dignity and great strength.

The former Pont Saint-Michel (Plate 120), built during the time the Pont Marie was under construction, is considered by de Dartein to be superior in design to the latter, which it resembled in many ways. Unfortunately, it was removed in 1857 and replaced by a new bridge to permit a widening and straightening of the street. Contrasting with the six years spent in building the old bridge, the new bridge was completed seven months after the old one was closed to traffic. The old Pont Saint-Michel was built more substantially than any of the other bridges of its time and stood without accident, requiring no such extensive reconstruction as the Pont-Neuf and the Pont Marie. The reason for this is evident. It was owned by the king and built by him at the expense of the concessionaire, a corporation which was to receive the revenue for a period of years. It was built under the direction of the same commission which had gained experience in directing the construction of the Pont-Neuf. The

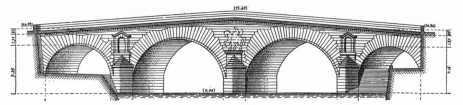

PLATE 120. Old Pont St. Michel at Paris. 1617–23. Reproduced from a drawing in "Études sur les Ponts en Pierre," by F. de Dartein.

Pont-Neuf and the Pont Marie had both been financed by the builder, the king in one case and the contractor in the other. The builders of both were over-anxious to save money.

The Pont Saint-Michel was built on the site of a former wooden bridge bearing two rows of houses which had several times been partially destroyed. A detailed specification was prepared by the commission and bids were taken from contractors. The work was started in 1617 and completed without difficulty in 1623. For the foundations, wood piles were driven close together to a firm foundation. Over these was spiked a wooden platform on which the masonry was laid. The specification required the stones of lower courses to be five or six feet long and from three to four feet thick, all clamped together with irons fastened into the stones with poured lead. Similar foundations had been used on other Renaissance bridges, the Rialto Bridge at Venice and the Pont des Boucheries at Nuremberg.

The Pont Saint-Michel had four spans with the roadway sloping up to the center pier with a grade of over six feet per hundred. The arches were in the form of circular arcs not quite full semi-circles, the span of the longer ones being about forty-six feet and the smaller ones at the end about thirty-three feet. The widest of the old Paris bridges, it was designed to carry two rows of houses, sixteen on each side, permitting a width of about thirteen feet to each house. Christofle Marie had offered to build the bridge with a double street and four rows of houses. His suggestion was rejected because it was considered that the great width of such a bridge would interfere with navigation, and the houses would obstruct the view over the river. In 1786, a general order was issued to remove all the houses from the bridges of Paris, but those of the Pont Saint-Michel stood until 1807 and 1808, when the road from Paris to Orléans was being improved.

The architectural treatment of the Pont Saint-Michel was very similar to that of the Pont Marie. The niches above the piers and the cornice were in better scale. The depth of the arch ring and the height of the spandrel wall above the arches were very great, giving the bridge a rather heavy appearance. The piers were set at a sharp angle with the roadway and the unsymmetrical treatment of the ends of the piers is interesting. In order to avoid a sharp edge at the springing of the arch, the arch stones were bevelled at one side of the span. The bevelled surface decreasing in width to a point at the opposite springing, resulted in a sort of one-sided corne-de-vache. De Dartein considers the Pont Saint-Michel one of the finest examples of Renaissance bridge architecture.

Of all the bridges of Paris, the first to resemble modern work in design and method of construction was the Pont Royal (Plate 121). Although built in the years from 1685 to 1687,

PLATE 121. Pont Royal, Paris, by Jules Hardouin Mansart and François Romain. 1685–87

PHOTO FROM "GRANDES VOÛTES" BY PAUL SÉJOURNÉ

Plate 122. Pont Royal, Paris

it is classed by de Dartein with the eighteenth century bridges because of its influence on later bridge building. It was designed by Jules Hardouin Mansart, the architect of the dome of the Invalides in Paris and many beautiful buildings. The construction was in charge of François Romain, a preaching brother, called from Holland because of his success in constructing the Pont de Maestricht.

Gauthey says* that Romain was called to the Pont Royal after the work had been started and serious difficulties had been encountered in founding the first pier from the right bank. In this connection, de Dartein argues that Romain was paid from the first of April, 1685, three weeks after the awarding of the contract, and therefore he must have been in charge of the work from its start. This makes the accuracy of Gauthey's description of the method of building the foundations seem uncertain. Gauthey wrote that three new processes were introduced by Romain: the preparation of the foundation by dredging, the use of pouzzolane cement, and the use of caissons or great timber boxes in which the masonry of the piers was built and sunk down on top of the piles. This latter would make Romain the inventor of caisson foundations, which have been generally accredited to the Swiss engineer Labélye, who used them for the Westminster Bridge in London, half a century later. De Dartein points out

* *Traité des Ponts,* Vol. I, page 69.

that the rapid progress with the work indicates that there was no serious accident, that Romain was in charge of the work from the start, and that the specifications for the bridge clearly described the use of the open cofferdams for which the conditions were entirely favorable.

The masonry foundations rest on piles cut off fifteen feet below the water level and capped with a wood platform. That was much deeper than usual at that time. According to the specifications, a cofferdam of double sheet piling filled with clay nine feet thick was built around the site of each pier and the water was then pumped out. This method is still extensively used for such foundations. It is better than the caisson method on account of the difficulty of getting uniform bearing for the caisson on the tops of all of the piles cut off under water.

The contract for the construction of the Pont Royal was awarded to Jacques Gabriel, architect to the king, who had done much of the work on the palace at Versailles and whose son became the first chief engineer of the Ponts et Chaussées. When Gabriel died in 1686, it was necessary for his widow to complete the contract. This she did with her brother Pierre de Lisle in charge and the construction was executed so successfully that it was completed in three years, the bridge being accepted officially by Libéral Bruant June 13 and 14, 1689.

The architecture of the Pont Royal set a new style for bridge design which was copied many times during the eighteenth century. The five arches are elliptical; the longest span is about seventy-seven feet. The width of the piers was only about one-fifth of the span, a proportion which was generally adopted after that, giving much more unobstructed waterway than had previous bridges. The elliptical arches are not as flat as those of the Trinita Bridge at Florence but still they appear light and graceful. The spandrels are entirely plain, without ornament except the cartouche at the crown of the center span. The cornice is a simple moulded band with a plain parapet. The cutwaters of the piers are sharply pointed and capped with stepped pyramids. The severity of the Pont Royal, which depends entirely on its form for its beauty, is typical of the civil architecture of the period of Louis XIV in which it was built, the period of classic architecture in France.*

The Renaissance was principally a period of architectural refinement in bridge design. Although the forms were new, the bridges were structurally about the same as the ones the Romans had built. The science of structural design had not yet been developed, and the practice of architecture included the design and supervision of such structures as bridges and sewers, as well as buildings. There was no distinction between the architect and engineer as

---

* Degrand mentions several other bridges which were built in Paris during the seventeenth century, the Pont au Double (1625–34), the former Pont Saint-Charles, built in 1606 and removed in 1852, the former Pont au Change (1639–47), replaced in 1859, and the Pont de la Tournelle, reconstructed in 1651 in the same style as the Pont Marie, and recently replaced with a concrete bridge faced with stone.

PLATE 123. Seventeenth-Century Bridge at Ronda, Spain

PHOTO BY VERNACCI, MADRID

PLATE 124. Puente de Toledo, Madrid, Spain. Sixteenth century

PLATE 125. Old Bridge at Elche, Spain

there is today. It was not until the eighteenth century, during which the École des Ponts et Chaussées was established in France, that engineering became a distinct profession. The extensive public improvements of technical nature undertaken then started an intensive specialization. This gradually has built up a science so involved and complicated, that engineers have neglected the study of architecture. The first effect on bridge design in the latter part of the eighteenth century was the modification of the style of the Renaissance bridges by the introduction of new structural principles. Since then many new principles have been discovered, and the study of their influence will show why bridges have not always been dutiful architectural subjects.

PART I · SECTION V

THE EIGHTEENTH CENTURY

THE EIGHTEENTH CENTURY

THE construction of the Pont Royal at Paris, toward the close of the seventeenth century, marked the beginning of a period of great activity in bridge building in France. Most of the Renaissance constructions were urban bridges required by the growth of the cities, while the medieval bridges or ferries still sufficed for the less important crossings. In 1716, the government Department of Bridges and Roads was organized of the graduates of the École de Paris, a technical training school, to direct the planning and building of complete systems of highways and canals in Central France. This work required the building of many new bridges.

During this century the development of the sciences, begun during the Renaissance, progressed with increasing rapidity. Because of the construction of canals, and the need of pumps and hydraulic machinery of various kinds, many experimental and theoretical studies were made and the science of hydraulics was put on a practical basis. The master bridge builder, Perronet, was also a builder of canals and the inventor of a number of hydraulic machines. Among the names of bridge builders of that period are those of such men as Chezy, and Pitot, familiar to every modern student of hydraulics.

During the first part of the eighteenth century, the French bridges* were similar in type to the Pont Royal, solidly built with simple monumental architectural treatment. It was during the construction of the bridge at Mantes that Perronet made the discovery which revolutionized stone bridge building, and resulted in the modern stone arch bridge. Later in the century, in the various provinces of France were built many bridges. These were remarkable for their beauty, the excellence of their construction, and for the boldness and originality of their design. In their decoration, a great variety of architectural forms was used with varying success. De Dartein gives excellent measured drawings of thirty-eight of these bridges.†

Bridge design remained in an experimental state, based on experience and judgment; but the general principles established by Perronet permitted him to build successfully stone bridges

---

* Among these are the bridges of Blois (by Gabriel in 1716), Compiegne (by Lahitte in 1730), Orléans (by Hupeau in 1751), Moulins (by Louis de Regemorte in 1756), Mantes (started in 1757 by Hupeau and finished by Perronet), and Tours (commenced by Bayeux in 1764 and finished by de Volgie).

† "Études sur les Ponts en Pierre."

PLATE 126. Bridge over the Cousin River near Avallon, France, by Antoine Puiné and Gauthey. 1786–90

which were as bold as any modern work. Also during Perronet's time, timber bridges of very long span were built in Germany. The 390-foot span at Wittengen credited to John and Ulrich Grubenmann, appears to be the longest wooden span ever attempted.

The greatest event of the eighteenth century, was the origin of the idea from which has grown the modern steel bridge. In 1755, an iron arch was cast and put together in a builder's yard in Lyon, France, but the bridge was never completed because of the great expense. About twenty-one years later, the first iron bridge was erected in England; and before the end of the century, iron had been used in a number of bridges in England and America. The application of iron to bridge building introduced many new and difficult problems. Economy in the use of this material demanded thin members proportioned according to mathematical rules not yet formulated in the eighteenth century; rules which have little in common with the laws of architectural design.

The simple structural form of the stone arch bridge is so satisfactory in itself, when the proportions are properly arranged, that beautiful designs have been produced during all the periods when good taste has prevailed. The iron or steel bridge has not always been so fortunate. The very first iron bridges were in the form of arches suggested by familiar structures and their appearance was pleasing. Later, new forms were invented in almost infinite variety to take advantage of the strength and lightness of the iron members. There was no artistic precedent for these new forms and they were quite frequently designed by engineers trained in mathematics but not in art. They considered economy of material second only to safety. The bridge of iron or steel has passed through an experimental period which has extended from that time to the present day. To the bridge engineer belongs the credit for the evolution of the great structures which play so important a part in modern life. The waywardness of the steel bridge as an architectural subject has been due to economic conditions, and to the necessity of technical specialization which has caused the engineer and the architect to follow distinctly separate paths.

With this general idea of the developments of the eighteenth century, it will be interesting to return to the study of some of the important bridges built during that time by the administrations of three different provinces of France: Centre, Languedoc, and Burgogne.

During the first part of the century, a number of large bridges were built in the central part of France, in the basins of the Seine and the Loire Rivers. There the influence of the Département des Ponts et Chaussées was strongest, combining as it did the skill of the most experienced bridge engineers. Considerable progress was made toward perfecting methods of construction and necessary equipment such as cranes, pumps, and pile drivers.

When the Corps des Ponts et Chaussées was established in 1716, Jacques Gabriel, architect to the king, was made the first chief engineer. He was the son of Jacques Gabriel who had started the construction of the Pont Royal, and of Marie Delisle, a niece of Jules Hardouin Mansart. He was the most famous of the Gabriels and the architect of many public buildings in Paris, Orléans, Lyon, Bordeaux and Rennes. On February 5, 1716, the old bridge at Blois was destroyed by flood. Gabriel's first act after his appointment was the building of a new bridge about two hundred and fifty feet above the former one.

The old bridge at Blois was one of the most picturesque of the medieval constructions. There were twenty unequal arches supported on piers of varying thickness and length. On the piers was a curious assortment of buildings. On the first pier next to the city and on the seventh from the other end were towers with draw-bridges and exterior stairways similar to those of the Pont Valentré. Two mills occupied five arches. Several other buildings, chapels or houses, stood on other piers. At the up-stream end of one of the piers rose an obelisque terminated by a globe bearing a cross, similar in form to the obelisque on the present bridge.

The construction of the new bridge at Blois was started the same year the old one was destroyed, and it was completed eight years later (Plate 127). Gabriel's ability as an architect is well shown by its design. It is severe and simple, similar to the Pont Royal in form, so skillfully proportioned that it forms a composition of remarkable beauty and interest. The largest of the old bridges of France, it has eleven elliptical arches, increasing in span and height with the rise of the roadway to the center of the bridge. The center span is about eighty-six feet and the end spans fifty-four feet, the slope of the roadway being about four feet per

PLATE 127. The Bridge at Blois, France, by Gabriel. 1716–24

hundred. The spandrels are perfectly plain with a simple moulded band at the sidewalk level and a plain solid parapet. The cutwaters are pointed up-stream with pyramidal caps, while the down-stream ends of the piers are three-sided.

In order to break the monotony of the eleven similar spans, the center three spans are grouped together by enlarging the piers which separate them from the rest of the bridge. The mid-point of the bridge is accented by sculptured cartouches placed at the crown of the center span, that on the up-stream side being surmounted by a well proportioned needle-shaped monument about forty-six feet high (Plate 128). This sculpture, by Gabriel and Guillaume Coustou, is very effective because of its location at the focal point of the composition, and its contrast with the plain surfaces of the rest of the masonry. The carving has almost escaped injury except for the defacement of the fleurs-de-lys during the Revolution.

The building of the foundations occupied three years. The piers were built on piles capped with timber platforms, the excavations being kept dry by cofferdams built around each foundation. The piles were about ten or eleven inches in diameter, placed about a foot and a half apart. They were driven to refusal with a ram raised by twenty to twenty-four men. The masonry was started on the wooden platform five or six feet below the water level, and the space between the cofferdam and the masonry was filled with stones.

PLATE 128. Cartouche at the Center of the Bridge at Blois, by Gabriel and Guillaume Coustou.

PLATE 130. Detail of Cartouche at Center of the Old Bridge at Orléans, France.

The bridge at Blois was so excellently built it would have stood without trouble if it had not unfortunately occupied a position of considerable military importance. In 1793 during the Guerre de Vendée, the third arch from the city was almost destroyed. Only a narrow strip of the arch was left, but it was sufficient to keep the span from collapsing, and it was repaired in 1804. Again in 1870, to prevent the German army from crossing, the span next to the center was mined and blown up. The other spans and the piers stood without injury in spite of a gap over sixty feet wide. Repairs were made in 1871 and 1872, and since that time it has been unmolested.

The bridge at Orléans, built from 1751 to 1761 by Hupeau, is of the same type as the Pont de Blois (Plate 129). The slope of the roadway is more gentle, the cutwaters are rounded instead of pointed, and the center of the bridge is decorated with a cartouche without the superimposed needle (Plate 130).

Shortly after the completion of the bridge at Blois, an unusually interesting little bridge was built near Juvisy on the national highway from Paris to Antibes (Plate 131). It is only a single span of about thirty-five feet. On account of its height above the water, seven narrow arches were thrown across the river at a lower level to sustain the high retaining walls.

PLATE 129. The Bridge at Orléans, France, by Hupeau. 1751–61

PLATE 131. The Pont des Belles Fontaines, near Juvisy, France. 1728

Gauthey* says that they were found necessary during construction because the walls were by mistake made too thin. Another writer, Louis Millin in 1790, describing the work in detail speaks as though the buttress arches were part of the original design. De Dartein points out that the walls show no evidence of displacement or other trouble and that the arches are built in with the walls; so that if they were not thus placed originally, the walls must have been torn down and rebuilt. However that may be, there was at least one unexpected development during construction. When the excavation was carried down to rock, a flowing spring of clear water was discovered, causing some difficulty. The builder cleverly took advantage of the spring by piping the water up to two monumental fountains placed at the center of the spans above each spandrel. The beautiful stone fountains were carved by Guillaume Coustou and

PLATE 132. Detail of Ornamental Fountains on the Pont des Belles Fontaines. From "Études sur les Ponts en Pierre," by F. de Dartein.

* *Traité des Ponts*, Vol. I, page 71.

PLATE 133. The Bridge at Saumur, France, by de Volgie. 1770

the bridge received the name of the Pont des Belles-Fontaines (Plate 132). The name of the designer of this bridge is not known, but de Dartein suggests that on account of its similarity in many respects to the Pont de Blois and on account of the importance of the bridge to the king, the work was probably directed by the Prémieur Ingénieur of the kingdom, Jacques Gabriel.

The bridge at Tours (1764–77) was one of the most imposing monuments of the time. It differed in some important respects from the bridges which have been described (Plate 11). The original design was made by Mathieu Bayeux in 1785; but, on account of the lack of funds and other difficulties, the construction was not started until six years later. Bayeux directed the work until 1774, when he was retired on account of old age and sickness. At that time, thirteen of the arches had been built. It appears that de Volgie, who succeeded Bayeux, made a new design for the upper part of the bridge and is responsible for the unusual and very successful decoration. It is very much like the bridge at Saumur which de Volgie completed in 1770 (Plate 133).

Contrary to custom, the roadway of the bridge at Tours is level and the fifteen nicely proportioned elliptical arches are of equal size and shape. The end spans are flared out so that the ends of the parapets are tangent to the quay walls. Back of these wing walls is a spacious plaza on each bank of the river. There is nothing to break the continuity of the bridge from bank to bank. Contrasting this structure with the one at Blois, de Dartein remarks: "We have the impression at Tours of a road, and at Blois of a bridge crossing a river." The individuality of the bridge at Tours is lessened in order to strengthen the continuity of the roadway. This effect is heightened by the subordination of the arches which are recessed in panels framed by the parapets and the ends of the piers. There is no projecting cornice; the parapets are set out beyond the plain spandrel walls, flush with the pilasters of the piers.

The specifications prepared by Bayeux for the bridge at Tours provided for the construction of the foundations with cofferdams and piles as used at Blois. Unfortunately, the recent successful use of caissons at Saumur influenced the engineers to use that method for five of the piers (the eighth to the twelfth) where the foundations were somewhat deeper. The construction of the foundations of the piers and abutments occupied seven years. Although carefully built, they have required extensive reconstruction. After the retirement of Bayeux, several disasters occurred.

In 1776, when the fourteenth arch was almost complete, the timber falsework, having been used for four other arches and weakened from age and handling, showed signs of failure. It collapsed while the work was being rushed to place the keystones to make the arch self-

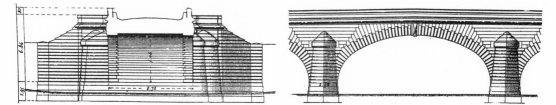

PLATE 134. Drawing of the Pont de Dizy, near Épernay, France, by Coluel and Lefebvre. 1767–73. Taken from "Études sur les Ponts en Pierre," by F. de Dartein.

supporting. The arch fell into the river, carrying the workmen with it. The next year, the eighth pier suddenly settled, destroying the two arches resting on it. This was one of the piers for which a caisson had been used. Perronet, who investigated the failure, reported that the dredging having been carried below the level of the top of the piles, the space between and around the piles had not been filled with stones and the unsupported piles bent over.

Again in January, 1789, the ice in the river having passed the bridges at Orléans and Blois, piled up against the bridge at Tours. This produced an undercurrent which washed out three of the piers where the piles were shortest, and destroyed the four arches farthest from the city. The rebuilding of these arches was not completed until 1810. That was not yet the end of the trouble, for in 1835, the cracking of the masonry indicated a settlement of the other piers founded on caissons. Soundings showed openings below the piers between the piles and these openings were pumped full of hydraulic lime mortar. The worst floods since 1840 have produced no further settlement. The engineers connected with the Pont de Tours had occasion many times to regret the economies which were practiced in its founding.

The Pont de Dizy near Épernay, France, built by Coluel and Lefebvre (1767–73) is interesting and beautifully designed (Plate 134). The arch stones are extended up into the spandrel wall as in the Pont Marie but the faces of the stones are bossed to represent an arch ring. This is rather curious because a true arch ring, free from the spandrels, would have been better construction than the false one. The arch, which carries the loads, should be free to move without carrying the vibration up through the spandrel walls.

These bridges just described which followed the Pont Royal were too early to be influenced by the discovery made by Perronet during the construction of the bridge at Mantes. This bridge, commenced by Hupeau in 1757, was a three-span structure very similar in form to the Pont Royal. The center span was 120 feet and according to the general rule then in use, the thickness of the piers was one-fifth of the span or twenty-four feet. It was considered that this thickness was great enough to permit the pier to act as an abutment and support an arch on one side without movement in case one of the arches resting on it was destroyed. Although a flat arch thrusting against the top of a high pier would require a much thicker pier to retain it than would an arch with high rise springing from the base of the pier, the same rule was applied to all bridges.

In 1763, when two arches at Mantes were under construction, one almost complete and the other just started, Perronet noticed that the thrust of the finished arch had caused a slight movement of the pier toward the other arch. He realized then that the pier was not strong enough to support the arch on one side only. He reasoned that to thicken the piers so that they would form abutments would be a waste of money, since many bridges of those proportions were standing satisfactorily. Since the arches must be depended upon to thrust against each other, the duty of the pier was really to support the vertical load, allowing the horizontal thrust to be carried through successive spans to the abutments at the end of the bridge. That being the case, the piers could be reduced materially in thickness without danger if the arches were of about equal span and were all in position before the falsework was removed. Reducing the thickness of the piers would also interfere less with the waterway, and lessen the danger of scouring of the foundations by the eddy currents created by the piers.

Perronet adopted these principles and reduced the thickness of the piers to about one-tenth of the span and even less in some cases. These new proportions meant, of course, that the destruction of one arch as occurred at Blois and Tours, would destroy the entire bridge. To prevent such action thick abutment-piers were sometimes placed at intervals in a long bridge to divide it into sections. At Blois, the two thick piers may have been used for purely architectural reasons, or the designer may have felt that the higher piers near the center of the bridge were not entirely safe in case of accident; but Perronet was the first to express such a principle.

In addition to making the piers thinner, Perronet also increased the waterway by raising the haunches and flattening the arches without raising the roadway. Probably the flattest arch built previous to that time was one of the spans of the Ponte Vecchio at Florence, where the rise of the intrados was one-seventh of the span. Perronet reduced this ratio to about one-twelfth in some of his work, although current practice was then one-third. One of the arches of the Pont de Saint-Dié (Plate 138), designed by a follower of Perronet, had a ratio of one-seventeenth. Not content with making the piers thin, Perronet also conceived the idea of economizing still further by reducing the piers to two flat columns with a space between bridged with a lateral arch. This was used for the bridge at Pont-Sainte-Maxence (Plate 135) and was proposed for the Pont de la Concorde at Paris but not adopted in the final plan. Divided piers were used later with separate arch ribs as in the case of Séjourné's Luxembourg bridge, but for solid arch barrels they have been abandoned.

PLATE 135. Perronet's Bridge at Pont-Sainte-Maxence, showing his use of narrow divided piers and flat arches. 1772–86.

Perronet's bridges were remarkably bold and efficient. At that time, it was necessary for the designs to be approved by the Assembly of the Corps des Ponts et Chaussées. He met with considerable opposition on account of the jealousy and conservatism of his contemporaries. This was natural because of his conspicuous position and radical ideas on bridge design. His career was a brilliant one. In 1725 at the age of seventeen, he had secured a position in the office of the Architect of the City of Paris, who then had charge of the roads and sewers as well as the buildings. Ten years later, he was admitted to the Corps des Ponts et Chaussées and appointed assistant engineer of the Généralité d'Alençon, of which he was made chief engineer after two years. This position he held for ten years, and did his work so well that he was called to Paris in 1747 to take charge of a school just established by the government for the purpose of training designers and map draftsmen. This was the beginning of the famous École des Ponts et Chaussées. By the same order, the king gave Perronet the general charge of the conduct and inspection of the work of the Ponts et Chaussées throughout the kingdom. He was made Inspector General in 1750 and, after the death of Hupeau in 1763, Prémieur Ingénieur des Ponts et Chaussées. From that time until his death in 1794, he planned and carried out many important works, the majority of which were in the Généralité de Paris.

After the completion of the bridge at Mantes in 1765, Perronet first applied his new theory of thin piers to the bridge at Neuilly, a suburb of Paris (Plate 136). This unprecedented bridge crosses the Seine with five arches of 120-foot span supported on piers thirteen feet thick. Perronet thus reduced the ratio of pier thickness to span length from the usual 1/5 to 1/9.3. He had not yet attempted his very flat arches and the rise of the elliptical arches at Neuilly is one-quarter of the span. This design was opposed in the Assembly, and even after its erection, one engineer, addressing the Académie des Sciences, prophesied its ruin and asked that guards be placed at the ends of the bridge to insure that carriages should pass over it slowly.

The river banks were improved with walks and ramps above the quays and with an open square at each end over the abutments. The bridge itself was almost without ornamentation but the parts were so well and gracefully proportioned that the architectural effect was excellent. The proportions of the spans have unfortunately been changed by the replacement of the solid parapet by an open iron rail in 1894.

The Pont de Neuilly was started in 1768 and completed in 1774. By that time, methods of constructing foundations were sure enough to justify the use of thin piers. Cofferdams were built of wood sheet-piling and clay around the site of each pier. Then the ground was excavated to a depth of about eight feet below the water level and the water was pumped out with a bucket-wheel operated by a paddle-wheel driven by the current. This was an invention of Perronet. Piles were then driven down to solid ground with drop hammers. The pile-driving records show that each of four hammers weighing from 1350 to 1740 pounds raised by twenty to thirty men drove $4\frac{1}{3}$ piles a day at a cost of thirteen livres, fifteen sols per pile. Other hammers raised by two horses drove $3\frac{1}{6}$ piles a day at a cost of five livres, one sol, seven

PLATE 136. The Pont de Neuilly over the Seine near Paris, by Perronet. 1768–74

[165]

deniers per pile. This detailed record indicates that engineers studied comparative costs as carefully then as they do now. The piles were cut off at a uniform height and an open grillage of timbers was fastened on them, the spaces between the pile heads and between the grillage timbers being filled with stone and mortar. On top of this solid platform, the heavy masonry of the piers was laid and carried up to the water level.

Since the arches depended on each other for support, it became necessary in 1772 to rush the work on the five arches so that all of the falsework could be removed together before winter. At one time, 872 men and 167 horses were engaged in building the bridge and transporting material. The centering was removed on September 22nd with unusual ceremony in the presence of King Louis XV and his entire court. All of the engineers in Paris assisted in the ceremony, dressed in the uniforms which the king had just accorded the Corps des Ponts et Chaussées. Louis XV, then sixty-two years old, had a great aversion for public ceremonies and his interest in the Pont de Neuilly was no doubt due to the fact that Perronet had been his playmate at Versailles when he was eight years old.

In 1771, Perronet made designs for the bridge at Pont-Sainte-Maxence and Nemours, and for his greatest work, the Pont de la Concorde at Paris. The bridge at Pont-Sainte-Maxence is the most perfect example of Perronet's innovations and the only one which combines flat arches and thin piers in the form of double columns (Plate 135). There are three arches of seventy-two-foot span with a rise of six feet five inches, the flattest arches that had ever been built. Because of the flatness of the arches, the mass of masonry forming the abutments extended back about fifty-six feet from the river. The stones of the piers were all clamped together with irons and the arches were so carefully built that when the French troops attempted to destroy the bridge with a mine in 1814, only a small part of one arch was blown out and the bridge was later repaired. About a hundred years later it was destroyed by the Germans.

The Pont Fouchard near Saumur was a very nicely proportioned bridge designed in 1772 by de Volgie, a pupil of Perronet (Plate 137). There are three arches of eighty-foot span with a rise of eight feet. The design of the abutments is interesting because de Volgie, not having any precedent to guide him and realizing that such flat arches exerted a tremendous pressure against the abutments, made an experimental model of stone of one of the arches. The model was built on a wooden form which could be lowered and the arch was loaded to determine the effect on abutments of different sizes. This bridge was the first of its kind to be completed (1783). The deflection of the arches due to the shrinking of the mortar joints caused a cracking and distortion of the parapets requiring their reconstruction.

PHOTO BY PAUL SÉJOURNÉ

PLATE 137. The Beautiful Pont Fouchard, near Saumur, France, by de Volgie. 1772–83

PHOTO BY LEVY & NEURDEIN

PLATE 138. The Flat Arch Bridge at Saint-Dié, France, by Lecreulx. 1785–1821

The bridge at Saint-Dié is the most daring of the flat-arch bridges although the spans are only thirty-six feet (Plate 138). The rise is only one-seventeenth of the span. The spans are given the appearance of straight slabs of stone by the curious bevelling of the arch stones at the spandrels. The bridge was designed by Lecreulx in 1785, but the construction was not started until 1804. Although it was small, the work progressed so slowly it was not finished until seventeen years later.

The Pont de la Concorde in Paris was Perronet's last and most important work (Plate 139). Occupying the most conspicuous place in the city, between the Chamber of Deputies and the Place de la Concorde, its name has been changed with each political upheaval. No agreement could be reached as to who should be honored by having their statues placed on its piers.

A model of the bridge done in plaster had been made by Perronet and presented to the king in 1772, but the work was not started until 1787. Then the north half of the Place de la Concorde, known at that time as the Place de Louis XV, was given over to the contractors for their temporary buildings and storage of materials. Perronet and his staff of engineers, draftsmen, and inspectors in charge of the construction lived in a pavilion previously occupied by Moreau, architect of the City, at the northwest corner of the Place. It was there that Perronet died in 1794, about a year after most of the work on the bridge had been completed.

PHOTO FROM "GRANDES VOÛTES" BY PAUL SÉJOURNÉ

PLATE 139. Pont de la Concorde, Paris, by Perronet. 1786–94

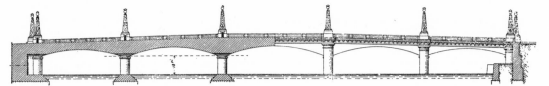

PLATE 140. Perronet's Original Design for the Pont de la Concorde. From a drawing in "Études sur les Ponts en Pierre," by F. de Dartein.

Perronet's first design for the Pont de la Concorde showed five flat arches with spans from seventy to eighty-eight feet, the rise being from 1/13.3 to 1/10.4 of the spans (Plate 140). Unlike most of the other bridges of that time, the roadway was not level but sloped up slightly toward the center span to give additional clearance for boats. The piers were to be nine feet thick, built in two parts as at Pont-Sainte-Maxence but the footing for each pier was to be continuous for the full width of the bridge. The ends of the piers were designed as round doric columns extending up to the roadway level. This introduced a difficult architectural problem because the short length and large diameter of the columns and the necessary lightness of the cornice over the spans required that the classical proportions be abandoned entirely. Perronet studied the decoration very carefully and produced a graceful, well proportioned design, worthy of its prominent position in the heart of one of the most beautiful capitals of Europe. He proposed placing over the piers, on pedestals forming part of the parapet, openwork bronze or iron pyramids supporting lamps. These were omitted because of the expense and the pedestals are still vacant. Unfortunately a number of changes were made from the original design.

Although Perronet was acknowledged to be the foremost authority on bridges, his radical appearing design for the Pont de la Concorde was severely criticized and political pressure was used to influence him to modify it. It must have hurt him deeply to be required to give up some of the ideas he was anxious to incorporate in his masterpiece, but he made the changes without complaint. The spans were lengthened slightly from the original project, the roadway was raised, increasing the rise of the arches, and the piers were made solid, although he successfully opposed their thickening. These modifications changed the proportions of the spans and made the spandrels higher at the haunches, detracting considerably from the grace of Perronet's first concept.

The beautiful parapet of the Pont de la Concorde, the first example of open balustrade used on a French bridge, is particularly interesting (Plate 141). In England, the balustrade of the old Westminster Bridge built in 1738–50 by Labélye set a style which was followed in several of the bridges over the Thames later in the eighteenth century. One feature of Perronet's

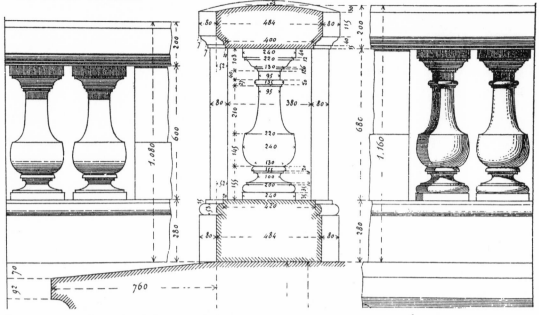

PLATE 141. Balustrade of the Pont de la Concorde. From a drawing in "Études sur les Ponts en Pierre," by F. de Dartein.

nicely detailed balustrade shows how carefully he studied the ornamentation. The balusters of the spans were round while those over the retaining walls of the quays were square and slightly shorter, giving them a more solid appearance appropriate to their position.

The foundations were constructed about as those of the Pont de Neuilly had been. At one time during the construction of the bridge, there were employed on the work as many as 1312 men, 58 horses, 11 barges and 14 small boats. To direct such a large enterprise at the time of the Revolution must have required considerable ability. Labor troubles were not very different from those of the present day. On one occasion, some of the workmen, receiving thirty cents a day, demanded forty cents and stopped work. The next day their wage was increased to thirty-five cents and they resumed work.

The eighteenth century bridges of the Province of Languedoc form an interesting contrast with those of Central France both in their design and in the method of construction. The École du Languedoc was not directly under the influence of the Corps des Ponts et Chaussées and there was no assembly to exercise control over bridge design. As a result, the technic of bridge building did not advance as rapidly in Languedoc as it did under Perronet in the Centre; but because of the absence of the standardizing influence of the Assembly, there resulted a greater variety of structural and architectural forms. While most of the bridges of the Centre were of the type of the Pont Royal, many of those of Languedoc were modeled after Roman bridges and some were reminiscent of the medieval gabled bridges.

In method of construction, there was more uniformity than in architectural form. Instead of founding the piers on piles cut off five or six feet below the water level as Perronet did, the engineers of Languedoc excavated inside of cofferdams down to solid bed and set the masonry of the piers and abutments directly on rock or hard-pan. Piles were used for temporary foundations of falsework and for cofferdams. The piers of the bridge at Gignac, for instance, were dug down through thick layers of sand and gravel to solid rock twenty-six feet below low water level. This was slower and more expensive than the use of piles but the results were more certain. It is said that this same method was used by the Romans in founding the Pons Cestius and the Pons Aelius in the Tiber.

Another remnant of Roman technic was the use of very thin mortar joints, sometimes less than one-sixteenth of an inch. This required very careful dressing of the stones but the reduction in the amount of mortar greatly decreased the settlement of the arch after completion and it was possible to build spans of nearly 160 feet as at Lavaur and Gignac with very little movement when the falsework was removed. The falsework was built as rigidly as possible to prevent settlement under the weight of the arch, and in the cases of the large arches just mentioned, the falsework was even built entirely of masonry with only enough blocks and wedges of wood at the top to permit a gradual removal of the support from the arch after its completion. Roman architectural details also appeared in some of the bridges such as the archivolt of uniform depth and the double cutwater as used at Toulouse.

The bridge built at Ornaisons by de Carney (1745–52) is a beautiful adaptation of the medieval gabled bridge with semi-circular arch (Plate 142). It has five spans and the architectural treatment of the 132-foot center span is particularly successful. The spandrels are perfectly plain with a half-round moulding serving as a cornice below a plain parapet. At the crown of the arch where the slopes of the roadway meet is placed a carved cartouche representing the cross of Languedoc surmounted by a crown. The result is an unusually beautiful composition which could not be improved by any added ornamentation.

The Pont d'Ornaisons was a bold construction for its time and was not built without disaster. The first design contemplated shorter spans. After the site had been selected where the bed-rock was near the surface, it was decided to change the location. Then after one of the main piers had been built, it was found that the ground where the next pier would come was insecure and de Carney was instructed to prepare a new design. A contract was awarded which required the contractor to complete the bridge within four years at a cost which should

PLATE 142. The Central Span of the Bridge at Ornaisons, France, by de Carney. 1745–52

not exceed 166,000 livres for any cause. Unfortunately for the contractor, the wooden false-work of the main arch collapsed suddenly before the arch was completed, causing the death of eleven men. The arch was finally built on new falsework designed by Pitot who used as a model the falsework built by Michael Angelo for the arch of St. Peters at Rome.

The aqueduct of Montpellier built by the great hydraulic engineer Pitot, is one of the finest works of the eighteenth century (Plate 143). It was designed to carry the water from the fountain of Saint-Clement to the Place du Peyrou and has a total length of nearly eleven miles of canal, tunnel and arcade. The stone arcade, about 4500 feet long, is of very fine construction modeled after the Pont du Gard near which Pitot had lived in his youth. The three arches at the end which join the aqueduct to the Chateau d'Eau are of special archi-tectural interest (Plate 144). They were designed by Giral and are ornamented to form a transition between the sober aqueduct and its elaborate terminal. The central span is finely detailed between two smaller arches more solid and severe. The aqueduct was started in 1752 and finished twenty years later.

The versatility of the engineers of Languedoc is well illustrated by the work of de Saget, aîné, who designed the Pont des Minimes over the canal at Toulouse, the Pont de Carbonne over the Garonne, and the Pont du Lavaur over the Agout. The three are widely different in

PLATE 143. The Aqueduct of Montpellier, by Pitot and Giral. 1752–72

PLATE 144. Detail of the Terminal Spans of the Aqueduct of Montpellier, by Giral

PLATE 145. The Pont des Minimes over the canal at Toulouse, France, by de Saget, aîné. 1760–63

form. The little Pont des Minimes of brick and stone is unusual because of the large scale of its decoration (Plate 145). The large cartouche at the center of the arch and the wide mouldings of the cornice are supported by strongly bossed vousoirs and quoin stones and the pronounced slope of the wing walls so that the effect is one of vigor rather than heaviness. The wing walls are in the shape of quadrants of circles in plan, a form frequently used in that province.

The Pont de Carbonne (1764–80) with three elliptical arches of about 100 to 111 feet, also of brick and stone is of simple, effective design. The abutments and piers are large and powerful, the piers having sharply pointed, two-staged cutwaters as at Toulouse.

The design of de Saget, aîné, for the Pont du Lavaur would have produced one of the finest and most imposing bridges of its kind. Unfortunately he died before its completion and his brother, known as de Saget, cadet, who succeeded him in charge of the work, simplified the cornice in a way that detracted considerably from its appearance. The single large arch of about 160-foot span is framed between enormous abutments in the form of round towers facing the river. The arch ring appears as a moulded archivolt of uniform width. The original design shows an attractive heavy cornice carried on modillions with a high parapet above (Plate 146). In actual construction, the cornice and parapet were reduced in size and the modillions eliminated, making the upper part of the masonry appear too shallow and light in proportion to the powerful arch. The Pont du Lavaur was built from 1769 to 1790.

A study of the French bridges of the eighteenth century would not be complete without a consideration of the remarkable structures built in the province of Bourgogne during the

PLATE 146. Original Design of the Pont de Lavaur, by de Saget, aîné. From "Études sur les Ponts en Pierre," by F. de Dartein.

last third of the century. Most of these were the work of Emiland Gauthey, one of the most active and able engineers of France. Gauthey was born in Chalon-sur-Saône. After studying mathematics at Versailles, and architecture in the atelier of Dumont, he entered the École des Ponts et Chaussées ten years after its organization. Having completed his studies there, he was appointed assistant engineer to the province of Bourgogne where he designed many important architectural and engineering works. He was later chief engineer of Bourgogne, and then Inspector General of the Ponts et Chaussées of France. Of all the accomplishments of his busy career, he was probably best known as the creator of the canal du Centre, and as the author of the "Traité de la Construction des Ponts." This was a general treatise on bridge design and construction, written just before his death. The "Traité" remained for many years the most complete and important work on the subject.

Gauthey's bridges were remarkable for their construction and for their great variety of well-studied ornamentation. De Dartein devotes an entire volume to his work. Gauthey showed great originality in decorating his bridges and produced some charming effects, although modern architects may question his taste in the selection of decorative motives. His sharp pyramids, columns, balls and eggs do not always appear appropriate on the bridge piers. He placed triangular panels surrounded by a plain band on the spandrels of several of his bridges and in some cases the panels were sculptured or set off by the use of different colored materials. Such panels can be applied in two ways, with the archivolt forming the lower band framing the panel, as on the Pons Palatinus in Rome; or better, with a separate band

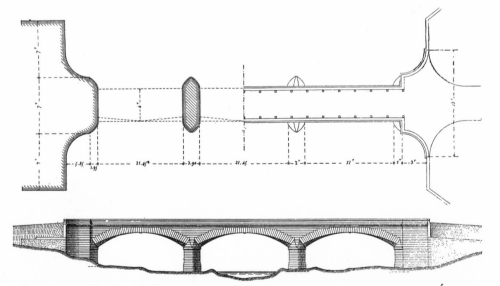

PLATE 147. The Pont de Homps, by Garipuy, fils, and Ducros. 1781–88. From "Études sur les Ponts en Pierre," by F. de Dartein.

PLATE 148. The Pont des Échavannes at Chalon, France, by Gauthey and Dumorey. 1781–90. From "Études sur les Ponts en Pierre," by F. de Dartein.

above the archivolt, as on the Ponte S. Trinita in Florence. Gauthey usually used the latter method, which is more satisfactory because the archivolt and spandrels really perform separate functions, and should not be combined in the panelling.

Regarding the construction of Gauthey's bridges, several things were of interest; particularly his method of building the foundations, the forms of the piers, and the construction of the arches with panelled soffits. Gauthey used a system for founding his piers which was very economical, and permitted accurate estimates of the cost to be made before the work was undertaken. This was a great advantage to both the owners and the contractors. In Gauthey's carefully formed opinion, this and other advantages outweighed the disadvantages. His method was as follows: The bed of the river at the site of the pier was first excavated as deeply as possible with a dredge. Piles were then driven and cut off fifteen to twenty-four inches below the low water level. Around the outside of the pier, sheet piling was driven and the space inside the sheet piling around the piles was filled with concrete deposited in the water. A timber grillage was next fastened to the tops of the piles, and concrete was rammed into the spaces between the grillage timbers. On top of the platform thus provided, only a few inches below the water level, the first course of the pier masonry was laid. A filling of stone was also placed around the outside of the foundations to prevent scouring by the currents. The foundations thus built were not always entirely successful. It was found in some cases that a lowering of the water level had permitted the timbers to rot, and that sometimes the concrete had not been properly placed around the piles. Two of his bridges were destroyed by floods because the foundations had not been carried deep enough.

The great care with which Gauthey designed his bridges is illustrated by the shape of his piers. He made experiments in a brook near his home. He determined that the best shape

PLATE 149. The Pont de Navilly on the Doubs River, by Gauthey. 1780. Up-stream side

PLATE 150. The Pont de Navilly, by Gauthey. Down-stream

for the cutwaters, separating the current with the least disturbance, was an ogival, or an elliptical curve, circumscribed on an equilateral triangle. In two of his bridges, at Navilly and at Guengnon, he continued the curve of the cutwater the full length of the piers, making them approximately elliptical in section. The soffits of the arches were curved in tangent to the side of the piers. This made the span of the arches shorter at the center-line of the bridge than at the spandrels, and greatly complicated the cutting of the stones.

Another interesting detail of five of Gauthey's bridges was the use of arch ribs. These were of dressed stone tied together horizontally with other ribs, forming recessed panels or coffers in the arch soffits, which were filled with masonry of smaller stones. Where the sides of the piers were curved, these ribs really simplified the construction; because the span of the ribs could be made to fit the piers, and the variation in span length could be taken up in the panels between the ribs.

The Pont de Navilly, Gauthey's masterpiece, with its rounded piers and abutments, prow-shaped cutwaters, coffered arches and carved ornamentation is unusually harmonious and attractive (Plates 149 and 150). The refinement of the design is remarkable. The continuous level roadway is carried over five equal spans with sturdy, gracefully shaped piers and abutments nicely related to the roadway, the river, and the river banks.

During the eighteenth century some important stone bridges were built outside of France, as the Westminster and Blackfriars bridges across the Thames in London. When the old London Bridge was no longer sufficient to carry the increasing traffic over the Thames, the Westminster Bridge was built (1738–50) by the Swiss engineer Labélye. This had semi-circular arches of about seventy-five-foot spans. It has since been replaced by a metallic bridge. Labélye is credited with the introduction of the caisson method of building foundations, which is said to have been first used on the Westminster Bridge.

The third bridge built across the Thames was the Blackfriars Bridge designed by Robert Mylne, architect and engineer. It was built from 1760 to 1769 and later replaced by iron arches. Elliptical arches were used there for the first time in England. Mylne was assisted in the design by Piranesi of Italy who made an engraved drawing for the bridge. The influence of Piranesi's drawings, which had a considerable effect on civic architecture and furniture design, was thus extended directly to bridge architecture. Among his many etchings of classical architecture are several of the Roman bridges, and some of his own design.

While the art of stone bridge building was being perfected in France, a new art was just being born. In 1776, before the construction of the Pont de la Concorde, an iron bridge was cast at the Coalbrookdale Iron Works under the supervision of Abraham Darby. This was

PLATE 151. First Iron Bridge at Coalbrookdale, England. 1776

erected across the Severn at Coalbrookdale where it was in service for more than a hundred and twenty years (Plate 151). It was a semi-circular arch of about 100-foot span. Apparently the next iron bridge was projected by Tom Paine, the son of a Quaker of Thetford. He emigrated to America and became interested in a plan for an iron bridge of 400-foot span across the Schuylkill at Philadelphia. He returned to England to have the span cast at Rotherham. The castings were successfully made and were exhibited in London; but the project was abandoned by Paine, who was attracted to France by the French Revolution. The material was reclaimed by the manufacturer and was used in a bridge built by Roland Burdon of Castle Eden, over the weir at Sunderland in 1796.

In 1796, Telford built his first iron bridge across the Severn, at Buildwar near Shrewsbury, England. The same year the first suspension bridge of the modern type with horizontal floor suspended from wrought iron chains was built in America by James Finley. He is credited with its invention.* The confidence which engineers felt in iron spans is shown by Telford's proposal in 1801, to replace the old London Bridge with a cast iron arch of 600-foot span. With the introduction of iron as a practical bridge building material, the stage was set for the spectacular developments of the nineteenth century.

* "Historical Sketch of the Successive Improvements in Suspension Bridges to the Present Time," by Charles Bender, *Transactions of the American Society of Civil Engineers*, 1868.

PART I · SECTION VI

MODERN BRIDGES

MODERN BRIDGES

THE modern science of bridge building is almost entirely a product of the nineteenth and twentieth centuries. The eighteenth century saw the perfection of the stone arch bridge and the introduction of iron as a competitor. Since then, stone arches have gradually fallen into disuse and the field has finally been captured by steel and concrete. In spite of the great scientific development, bridge building as an art, having passed through a period of actual depression, stands about where it did during the eighteenth century. For that reason the work of the nineteenth century, while of great interest to the scientist, is less attractive to the artist. The twentieth century work is of great interest to both because of the attempts made to beautify the scientifically designed bridges. The results obtained in many cases show that architectural design has been greatly complicated by the introduction of the new materials and scientific principles. The experimental period has not yet been passed.

Aside from economic conditions which have often demanded absolute minimum cost, the

PHOTO BY JUDGES, LTD.

PLATE 152. Royal Border Bridge, Berwick-on-Tweed. Early stone railway viaduct

PHOTO BY WEHRLI-VERLAG

PLATE 153. The Ruseinviadukte of the Rhätische Bahn, Switzerland

PLATE 154. The Old Iron Viaduc de Grandfey, near Fribourg, Switzerland. Built 1857–62, and recently replaced by concrete viaduct without interrupting traffic.

PLATE 155. Waterloo Bridge, London, by John Rennie. 1809–17

judgment of modern designers has been affected by a tenacious belief that the most economical and scientific design is the most attractive appearing. Although that is not true, there is some truth behind it; just enough perhaps to make it dangerous, for structural efficiency is a necessary aid to beauty.

The complete story of modern bridges, if such a thing could be unraveled, would be too complicated to interest the general reader. The designer of bridges can find as much detailed information as he needs in text books, so only an outline will be given here.

Early in the nineteenth century, a new factor greatly stimulated bridge building. The new railroads built during this time of unusual industrial expansion required a multitude of bridges. Where formerly a prominent bridge engineer built only a few bridges in his entire career, those in charge of the railroad construction, as the Stevensons in England, built many in a short time. The Newcastle and Berwick Railway alone required one hundred and ten. Railways were much more exacting than highways. They demanded that the tracks be almost level and they required rigid supports for comparatively heavy loads. Great arcaded stone structures had previously been built to carry aqueducts across valleys, and somewhat similar structures with heavier arches and piers were now built to carry the railways. Many such stone viaducts were built in England and other European countries. In England, cast iron railroad bridges also became common while in America most of the bridges were of timber.

The use of stone as a material for bridge building continued through the nineteenth century. A great many large bridges were constructed of that material. Perhaps on account of their number they lack somewhat the interest of the earlier bridges, and only a few of them will be mentioned here.

In England, John Rennie, famous as a builder of docks, canals, and lighthouses, as well as bridges, built the Waterloo Bridge, the fourth bridge across the Thames in London, from 1809 to 1817 (Plate 155). His next bridge was the Southwark Bridge also across the Thames in London, in 1819. It had cast iron arches with a center span of 240 feet, a remarkably bold structure at that time. The new London Bridge was designed by George Rennie, the son of John Rennie, and built by Sir John Rennie, his brother (1824–31, Plate 156). The high stone viaducts of Mouse-Water and Edinburgh were built about the same time, the former in 1822, and the latter in 1831.

The stone and brick bridge at Bordeaux was the most important work of the early nineteenth century in France (Plate 157). It was successfully completed in 1822 over the Garonne at a location where deep shifting sands had previously discouraged bridge builders from making any attempt. In Italy, a large stone arch bridge was completed in 1834 over the Dora

PLATE 156. The New London Bridge. 1824–31

PLATE 157. The Bridge over the Garonne at Bordeaux, France, completed in 1822

PLATE 158. The Pont Mosca at Turin, Italy. 1834

River at Turin, by Mosca, who had studied at the École des Ponts et Chaussées at Paris (Plate 158). This single flat span of nearly 150 feet was evidently inspired by the work of Perronet.

Although comparatively few stone bridges were built in the United States, there were some notable structures such as the Carrollton Viaduct of the Baltimore and Ohio Railroad (1829, Plate 159); the Thomas Viaduct over the Patapsco on the Baltimore and Washington

PLATE 159. One of the first stone arch railroad bridges in America, the Carrollton Viaduct on the Baltimore & Ohio Railroad. 1829.

[188]

PLATE 160. High Bridge, New York City, by John B. Jervis. 1839–48

PLATE 161. The Pont Adolphe at Luxembourg, by Paul Séjourné. 1899–1903

PLATE 162. The Pont des Amidonniers over the Garonne at Toulouse, France, by Paul Séjourné. 1903–11.

Railroad, built by B. H. Latrobe; the Rochester Canal Aqueduct-bridge; the Cabin John Bridge at Washington; and the Aqueduct or High Bridge of New York City. Of these, the last two are the most widely known.

The Cabin John Bridge has a single arch of about 218-foot span built by General Meigs (1857–64) to bring a watersupply to the City of Washington. Until the construction of the Luxembourg arch in 1903, it was the longest masonry span in the world.

High Bridge, near 174th Street, New York, was erected by John B. Jervis, a builder of railroads and Chief Engineer of the Croton Aqueduct Commission, to carry the Croton Aqueduct across the valley of the Harlem River to Manhattan Island (Plate 160). With high solid piers and semi-circular arches in the monumental style of the old Roman bridge across the Tagus at Alcantara, it has been considered the finest old masonry structure in America. The popular sentiment for High Bridge was shown by the storm of protest aroused a few years ago when its removal was recommended by the War Department because its piers obstructed the main channel of the river. As a result, four of the piers and five arches have been replaced by a steel arch span of 426 feet, the rest of the monument being preserved in its original form (Plate 364).

The final development in stone bridge design was the use by M. Paul Séjourné, the celebrated French bridge engineer, of two separate arch ribs, side by side, with the roadway carried on columns. This arrangement was first used in Séjourné's Pont Adolphe over the Petrusse at Luxembourg (1899–1903, Plate 161). It was a daring design with a span of nearly 280 feet, the longest in the world at that time. The roadway was built of reinforced concrete supported on stone columns over the arches. This bridge was copied in concrete by the designers of the Walnut Lane Bridge in Philadelphia and the form is now commonly used in concrete bridge construction (Plate 292). The elimination of much of the masonry from the arch ring and the omission of the heavy filling above the arch greatly reduced the cost of large, high spans. At the completion of the Luxembourg Bridge, M. Séjourné commenced the construction of another large bridge of the same type over the Garonne at Toulouse, finished in 1911 (Plate 162).

The construction of bridges with separated stone ribs and concrete roadways marked the beginning of the end of stone bridge construction. The next step was the replacement of the stone masonry of the arches with concrete, producing the all-concrete bridge. On account of its lower cost, greater adaptability to any form desired, and greater speed of construction, concrete has practically displaced stone as a structural bridge material. Stone is now usually limited to facing and architectural features.

Wood is not generally considered a suitable material for bridge building today. Few people realize what an important part the wooden bridge played in the development of the American continent. When American wooden ships ruled the seas, great bridges of timber were carrying her railroads and highways through undeveloped forests. American bridge engineering was described in a very interesting manner in 1859 by an English engineer, David Stevenson, who made a tour of inspection of the country and wrote as follows: *

"The vast rivers, lakes and arms of the sea in America which have been spanned by the bridges are on a scale which far surpasses the comparatively insignificant streams of this country, and, but for the facilities afforded for bridge building by the great abundance of timber, the only means of communication across most American waters must have been by means of a ferry or a ford. The bridge over the River Susquehanna at Columbia, and that over the Potomac at Washington, for example, are each one mile and a quarter in length; and in the neighborhood of Boston there are no less than seven bridges, varying from 1500 feet to one mile and a half in length. The bridge over Lake Cayuga is one mile, and those at Kingston on Lake Ontario, and at St. John's on Lake Champlain, are each more than one-third of a mile in length.

"The American bridges are in general constructed entirely of wood. Although good building materials have been plentiful in every part of the country, the consumption of time and money attending the construction of a stone bridge of so great extent must, if not in all, at least in most cases, have proved too considerable to warrant their erection. Many of those recently built, however, consist of wooden superstructure resting on stone piers, and in general exhibit specimens of good carpentry, and not infrequently good engineering."

Of the bridge over the Susquehanna at Columbia (1832–34) he says: "It certainly is a magnificent work, and its architectural effect is particularly striking. It consists of no fewer

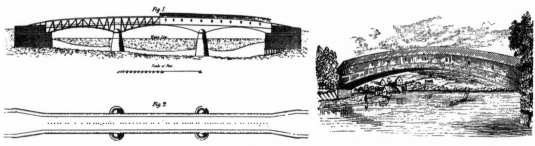

FROM "THE CIVIL ENGINEERING OF NORTH AMERICA" BY DAVID STEVENSON

PLATE 163. Timber Bridge over the Schuylkill at Philadelphia

PLATE 164. The "Colossus Bridge" at Philadelphia

* "The Civil Engineering of North America," by David Stevenson, 1859, Chap. VII.

PLATE 165. Old Iron Bridge over the Wye, Chepstow

than twenty-nine arches of 200 feet span, supported on two abutments and twenty-eight piers of masonry, which are founded on rock at an average depth of six feet below the surface of the water. The waterway of the bridge is 5800 feet; and its whole length, including piers and abutments, is about one mile and a quarter. The bridge is supported by three wooden arcs, forming a double roadway which is adapted for the passage both of road and railway carriages. There are two footpaths, which make the whole breadth of the bridge thirty feet.

"There is another bridge over the Schuylkill at Philadelphia consisting of a single arch of no less than 320 feet span, having a versed sine of about thirty-eight feet* (Plate 164). This bridge has a breadth of roadway of about thirty feet. It has been erected for several years, and is in good repair and constant use."

While these enormous wooden bridges were being built in America, the English engineers were experimenting and developing iron bridges of different types. The cast iron bridge passed through various stages, from the thin arched ribs of the Coalbrookdale bridge to the solid arch ring carrying the roadway on vertical columns, as in the later bridges. An attractive little iron bridge was built at Bettws-y-Coed, Wales, with the words "This Arch Was Constructed in the

---

* This bridge, known as the "Colossus Bridge," had a clear span of 340 feet and was erected in 1812 by Lewis Wernwag. It was burned in 1838 and replaced by a 358-foot suspension span by Charles Ellet. Stevenson had seen the "Colossus" on a previous visit to America.

PLATE 166. Waterloo Bridge at Bettws-y-Coed, Wales

PLATE 167. Menai Bridge, Wales, by Thomas Telford. 1820–26. 570-foot span

Same Year the Battle of Waterloo was Fought," cast into the arches (Plate 166). About the same year, 1815, Telford designed the suspension bridge across the Mersey at Runcorn directing public attention to that type of bridge, saying that it had been used in America and India. The suspension bridge across Menai Straits was designed in 1818 and built two years later (Plates 167 and 168). During its construction the Conway Castle bridge was started (Plate 169). These early suspension bridges were built with wrought iron chains. The first steel eyebar chains were used by Mitis in 1828 for the 300-foot suspension bridge at Vienna, Austria. Steel was not used again for many years because of its high cost. The chain suspension bridge at Budapest was built in 1846;

PHOTO BY UNDERWOOD & UNDERWOOD

PLATE 168. Roadway of the Menai Bridge

and the 870-foot span at Fribourg, Switzerland, from 1832 to 1835 (Plate 171). This latter bridge, 168 feet above the water, has four wire cables instead of eyebar chains.

The pioneer development of the suspension bridge took place in America. It required considerably less iron than the cast iron arch bridge, and the roadway was built of wood. From 1796 to 1808, forty-eight suspension bridges were built following Finley's patent. The largest of these was the Schuylkill chain bridge of three hundred and six-foot span.* Finley's bridges were built with wrought iron chains. The use of wire cables to suspend bridges is also said to be an American invention, the first one being the four hundred and eight-foot span at Philadelphia, built before 1808. French engineers also played an important part in the development of the wire suspension bridge. The modern method of spinning the cables in place was originated by Vicat in 1831, for a bridge across the Rhone and was later adopted at Niagara and Cincinnati by Roebling.

The difficulties experienced with the early suspension bridges were clearly described by Whipple in his "Essay on Bridge Building," written in 1847. He said: "Suspension bridges have been used with tolerable success for common travel, where the moving load is trifling

* "Historical Sketch of the Successive Improvements in Suspension Bridges to the Present Time," by Charles Bender, *Transactions of the American Society of Civil Engineers*, 1868.

PLATE 169. Conway Castle Bridge, Wales

PLATE 170. Clifton Suspension Bridge

PLATE 171. The Old Suspension Bridge at Fribourg, Switzerland, by Chaley. 1832–35

compared with the weight of the structure itself. The most important now in use in this country is that over the Schuylkill near Philadelphia, being 343 feet long and 27 feet wide. It is sustained by wire cables passing over towers at the corners of the bridge, the ends of the cables carried down obliquely and anchored into the ground outside of the towers, and the central portions hanging in a catenarian curve between the towers. The roadway or platform is suspended from these curved cables. This is the general plan of constructing suspension bridges, using sometimes wire cables, and sometimes chains formed by connecting bars of iron. Much longer ones have been constructed in Europe, even two or three times as long as the Schuylkill bridge, some of which have endured while others have failed."

Whipple continues: "A serious difficulty in the use of suspension bridges is the want of fixedness or stability among the parts. The curve of the chains being left to find its own equilibrium yields to every force that tends to disturb that equilibrium, and hence arises an undulatory motion whenever the bridge is exposed to the passage of heavy loads, or to the action of strong winds, which is frequently attended with disastrous consequences. This quality renders these bridges utterly unfit for railroad purposes, as they are usually constructed. No plan has yet, as I believe, been devised and successfully executed, to obviate the difficulty." This difficulty is overcome in modern suspension bridges by the use of stiffening trusses placed along the roadway of the span suspended from the cables in order to prevent the distortion of the cable curve. Because of their flexibility, suspension bridges are not generally suitable for railroad loading.

Roebling's wire cable suspension bridge across the Niagara River with a span of 821 feet was built in 1855. While this was being planned, Whipple said that he doubted the success of such a suspension bridge which was to be stiffened with an arch. He suggested the use of a deep truss with the railroad track on top and the highway below the track between the trusses. In his words: "The passageway for carriages and common travel could be arranged underneath perfectly secure from all dangers except perhaps, that of frightening horses by the passage of trains overhead. It would probably be best, however, not to suffer horses to go on to the bridge when trains were in hearing."

Whipple's book also throws an interesting light on the question of materials for bridge building in the nineteenth century. In 1847 he wrote: "Wood and iron, as before mentioned, are the only materials that have been employed in bridge building (I refer only to the superstructures) to any extent worthy of notice, and it seems reasonable to conclude that on these, we must place our dependence.

"Cast iron will resist a greater crushing force than any other substance whose cost will admit of its being used as a building material. Steel has a greater power of resistance, but its cost precludes its use as a material for building. Wrought iron resists nearly equally with cast iron, but its cost is twice as great, which gives cast iron entirely the advantage. On the other hand, wrought iron resists a tensile force nearly four times as well as cast iron, and twelve or fifteen times as well as wood, bulk for bulk.

"Not only are these the strongest materials, but they are also the most durable. In fact with proper precautions they may be regarded as imperishable.

"It would seem, then, that wrought iron for tension and cast iron for thrust, were the best materials that could be employed for building bridges. But wood, though greatly inferior in strength and durability, is much cheaper and lighter, so that making up with quantity for its want of strength, and by frequent renewals for its want of durability, it has hitherto been almost universally used in this country for bridge building, and in the scarcity of means, and the unsettled state of things, in a new country where improvements are, necessarily, to a great extent of a temporary character, this is undoubtedly the most economical material for the purpose.

"But it is believed that the state of things has now assumed that degree of settled permanency in many parts of this country, and available means have accumulated to that extent which renders it consistent with true economy to give a character of permanence to our improvements, and in the erection of important works, to have more reference to durability, even at the cost of greater present outlay; and in this view of the subject, it seems highly probable that one of the channels in which this tendency of things will develop itself will be in the extensive employment of iron in the construction of important bridges."

Some years later, in 1869, Whipple said: "The want of confidence which existed in the public mind a few years ago, as to the safety of Iron Bridges for Railroads and other purposes, having mostly yielded before the light of experience, it is now not necessary to make use of argument in favor of such structures.

"There is still, however, a lurking doubt as to the propriety of the use of Cast Iron in bridges, so there may be said to be two Schools or parties of the advocates and builders of Iron Bridges; one in favor of a combination of Wrought & Cast Iron, and the other, advocating the use of Wrought Iron exclusively, in Iron Bridge Construction."

Thus the use of iron was introduced into American bridge building. In 1855, the Bessemer process for making steel cheaply was invented, and the more reliable Siemens-Martin open hearth process soon after. The development of the steel industry was very gradual, however, and steel did not entirely replace wrought iron until about the last decade of the century. The first important American bridge of steel was the Eads Bridge at St. Louis (Plate 172). The story of the financial and technical difficulties overcome by Captain Eads in its building is a thrilling one. For the deep foundations of its piers, the pneumatic caisson process was used for the first time in America. Its arches of special crucible steel were erected without false-work below in the river, by the cantilever method, again used a few years ago for the erection of the Hell Gate Bridge in New York (Plate 173).

Iron permitted a much greater variety of forms for bridges than did stone; and when it was found that arches and suspension systems of iron were not suitable in all locations, various forms of girders and trusses were invented.

Robert Stevenson's original plan for the Britannia Bridge at Menai, Wales (designed in 1847), called for two cast iron arch spans of 350 feet each. The Admiralty rejected this design because the center pier would interfere with navigation, and it would not permit falsework to be placed in the channel during the erection of the bridge. The suspension bridge was not considered strong enough for railroad traffic. Stevenson finally decided to use large wrought

PLATE 172. Eads Bridge, St. Louis. 1868–74

PLATE 173. Erection of the Hell Gate Arch by the Cantilever Method. 1915

iron girders built in the shape of tubes of iron plates with the greater part of the metal in the roof and floor (Plate 174). There were two tubes, side by side, each carrying a track. Stevenson had tests made to determine the strength of iron and also built a model of the tubular bridge and tested its strength. Influenced either by lack of perfect faith in his design or by the criticism of other engineers, he built the towers high enough to permit the attachment of suspension chains to reinforce the tubes if they should be found insufficiently strong. This was probably due to his habitual caution in such matters as illustrated by an incident related by Smiles in his "Lives of the Engineers."

The tubes were floated between the piers and raised with hydraulic jacks. When ready, Stevenson's field engineer reported that the tubes could be raised in a day or two. He replied, "No. You must only raise the tube inch by inch, and you must build up under it as you rise. Every inch must be made good. Nothing must be left to chance or good luck." The wisdom of this was proved one day when the bottom burst from one of the hydraulic jacks while it was at work. The tube fell about nine inches crushing solid castings like nut shells. The tube was slightly strained and deflected but still serviceable. Stevenson also erected a tubular bridge in America, the Victoria Bridge over the St. Lawrence at Montreal (1854–60). It was so expensive that it was not approved by American engineers and it was not repeated.

PLATE 174. Brittania Bridge at Menai, Wales, by Robert Stevenson. 1850

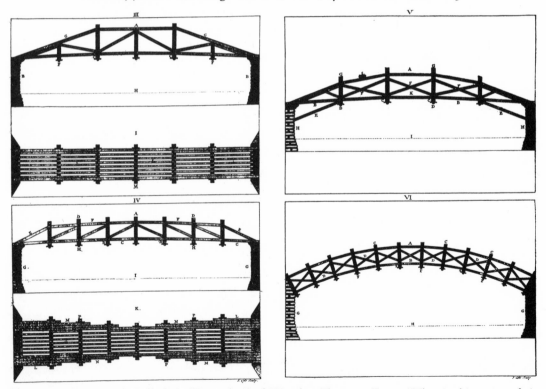

PLATES 175 AND 176. Palladio's "Draughts" of Wooden Trusses. From "The Architecture of A. Palladio," by Giacoma Leoni.

It was necessary to keep a gang of riveters constantly at work renewing defective rivets and after a few years it was replaced by a more modern bridge.

The design of the early girder and truss bridges of wood and iron was based on experience with previously built bridges or with specially built small scale models which were loaded to determine what weights they would support. Palladio, who is credited with developing the bridge truss, wrote in the sixteenth century: "But because the particulars are infinite, no certain or determinate rule can be given about them, and therefore I shall present you with some draughts, and specify their proportions, whereby everyone, as occasion offers, or his genius is happy, may take his measures and perform what shall be worthy of praise" (Plates 175 and 176). Palladio's draughts of trusses show that he understood the principle of dividing the trusses into triangular panels, but he had no idea of the size of the stresses carried by the individual members. He used the same size timbers for all verticals and diagonals. In some cases he even increased the top and bottom horizontal members from the center to the end, although the greatest stress in the horizontal members is at the center. It was not until about the middle of the nineteenth century that the correct theory of truss design was developed so that each member of the truss could be proportioned for the actual stress according to the strength of the material used. In 1847, Squire Whipple published his book on bridge building which gave a rational method of truss design for the first time.

Even the strength of simple beams of uniform cross section resting on supports at each end had been the subject of much speculation and controversy for a long time. Apparently no progress toward the solution of this problem was made until the seventeenth century. In 1638, Galileo stated a law of stress in beams, but unfortunately, it was incorrect. In 1678, Hooke announced his law of proportionality of stress and strain, which said in substance that within a certain limit called the elastic limit, the deformation of a piece of material is proportional to the load. This discovery made experimental work possible and in 1680, Marriotte proved that the fibers in the top of a simple beam are in compression and those in the bottom are in tension. He also correctly assumed that at a surface passing through the center of gravity of the cross section, there is neither tension nor compression. The magnitude of these tensile and compressive stresses was still not discovered for many years. In 1713, Parent announced that the total compressive stress is equal to the total tensile stress on any cross section, and the same fact was again stated independently sixty years later by Coulomb. Beam design was finally put on a practical basis in 1824 by Navier and about the same time Eaton Hodgkinson, who had done much experimental work on strength of materials in England, published a sim-

PLATE 177. Brooklyn Bridge, by John A. Roebling, completed in 1883. Main span 1595 feet

PLATE 178. Philadelphia-Camden Bridge, completed in 1926. Main span 1750 feet. Board of Engineers: *Ralph Modjeski, Chairman; George S. Webster and Lawrence A. Ball. Paul P. Cret, Consulting Architect.*

ilar treatment. A complete and accurate treatise on beam design was published in 1857 by Saint-Venant, a pupil of Navier.

The strength of the columns was determined experimentally. Euler published his theoretical formula for long columns in 1744, and in 1840, Eaton Hodgkinson determined by tests the constants to be used with Euler's formula. Since then various formulas for the strength of columns have been derived from tests.

The theory of design of such complicated structures as arches, continuous beams and trusses, and stiffened suspension bridges, was not developed until the latter part of the nineteenth century. These are known as statically indeterminate structures because the stresses in their members cannot be determined by the simple law of statics. This law is based on the fact that when a body is not in motion, all of the forces acting on it are balanced. With such structures, it is necessary to assume a preliminary design and investigate the elastic deformations of the various parts, in order to compute the actual stresses. The theory of stiffened suspension bridges was developed after the Brooklyn Bridge had been designed by John A. Roebling (Plate 177). That remarkable structure, with an unprecedented span of 1595 feet, has been in use since 1883 under loads much greater than had been anticipated. With the 3500-foot span of the Hudson River Bridge at New York under construction, and still longer spans proposed, the suspension bridge has grown to proportions which would never have been credited by the master bridge builder of the eighteenth century.

So rapid and complete was the development of the science of bridge engineering during the nineteenth century, that the twentieth century engineer has found himself well equipped to create the tremendous long-span bridges which are so well known today. Advances have been

PLATE 179. End of One of the Main Cables of the Philadelphia-Camden Bridge

PLATE 180. Cappelen Memorial Bridge, Minneapolis. 400-foot central span; completed in 1923. *N. W. Elsberg, City Engineer; K. Oustad, Bridge Engineer.*

made during the last thirty years; but they consist largely in refinements of theory and processes of manufacture, rather than the discovery of new and fundamental principles unthought of before.

Concrete has recently become one of the most important of bridge building materials although the first modern bridge of concrete was built not long before the close of the nineteenth century. This rapid development was made possible by the previously accumulated mathematical theories, and well equipped testing laboratories. When the new material was introduced, it was studied in the light of all previous experience and much has been learned about its possibilities. Reinforced concrete combines many of the desirable characteristics of stone, steel, and wood. Its adaptability to beautiful architectural treatment is shown by many recent bridges.

No attempt will be made to name or describe the many types of bridges used in modern practice because the distinctions are too technical and involved to be of general interest. Each type has special characteristics which fit it for use in certain locations. Since no two bridge sites are just alike, there result modifications of each type, until the variety of designs is almost infinite. This, and the fact that there are constant advances through experience and research,

[206]

PLATE 181. The Grandfey Viaduct, near Fribourg, Switzerland. *Adolph Bühler, Bridge Engineer, Schweizerischen Bundesbahnen.*

PLATE 182. The Pont de Pérolles, Fribourg, Switzerland. 1924. *Jaeger & Lusser, Engineers; Frölich, Broillet et Genoud, Architects; Zublin et Cie, Contractors.*

PLATE 183. The Pont de Zähringen, Fribourg, Switzerland. 1924. *Jaeger & Lusser, Engineers; Zublin & Cie, Contractors*

PLATE 184. Tunkhannock Viaduct of the Delaware, Lackawanna & Western Railroad, Nicholson, Pa. Built 1912-15. G. J. Ray, Chief Engineer; A. B. Cohen, Bridge Engineer; Flickwir & Bush, Contractors.

make bridge engineering one of the most fascinating of professions. The importance of bridges in our modern systems of transportation and communication, justifies the expenditure of great sums of money for substantial permanent bridges. The conditions which produced the stark temporary structures of the last century have changed. There is no longer reason for withholding beautiful forms.

PART II · SECTION I

INFLUENCE OF MATERIAL

ON BRIDGE FORMS

INFLUENCE OF MATERIAL
ON BRIDGE FORMS

THE illustrations of Part II have been carefully selected from a collection of several thousand photographs to show the variety of beautiful forms that have evolved from the elementary beam, arch, and cable of primitive times. They are presented with the hope that each detail, either good or bad, will be carefully studied and criticized by designers of bridges; so that new bridges may profit by the successes and failures of the old, and be more beautiful.

The bridges are classified here according to the materials of which they are made because the qualities of each material have a definite influence on the forms into which it can be built. Without going deeply into the subject of structural mechanics, there are two elementary kinds of stress to be resisted by a bridge material: tension, which exists in the cable of a suspension bridge, and compression, which is illustrated by the action of an arch or column. The bending of the beam or truss is a combination of tension on one side and compression on the other. The top of a simple beam or truss is in compression and the bottom is in tension. Some materials are better suited to one kind of stress than another, and it is principally that characteristic which determines the form of the bridge.

*   *   *   *

Stone masonry is suited only to compressive stresses and can therefore be used only for arch spans (Plate 186). Separate stones have sometimes enough tensile strength to permit their being used for beams and slabs as seen in the clapper bridges, and small Japanese garden bridges (Plates 28, 29 and 185).

Stone is frequently used in modern bridges for architectural purposes to encase steel towers, or concrete arches, and piers. Concrete bridges enclosed with stone are classified here as stone bridges, because architecturally they are of stone. The concrete structures may not have the proportions of stone bridges. Such composite bridges must be carefully designed so that the stonework will not appear illogical or incongruous.

PLATE 185. Japanese Garden Bridge. Curved slabs of stone

Concrete piers are often faced with granite to protect them from the disintegrating effect of freezing and thawing of the water at their bases.

*   *   *   *

Wood will resist either compression or tension and single pieces are suitable for use as beams. The timber bridges of Bhutan and Cashmere are cleverly contrived of timber beams put together so as to span wider streams than could have been crossed by the available single sticks (Plates 31, 32, 225 and 226).

The greatest weakness of timber as a bridge building material lies in the difficulty in connecting together separate pieces. Another material, such as iron, must be used to fasten timbers together to form trusses; and even then it is impossible to make a joint which will be as strong as the timber in tension. Wood is therefore more suitable for compression than tension, and some of the old timber trusses had iron tension members.

The unique Kintai Kyo of Japan (Plate 189) and the footbridge at Cambridge (Plate 211) are arch bridges of timber. Many of the early American timber bridges consisted of arches stiffened with trusses.

Wood is also suitable for posts and piles, and one of the most important forms of wooden bridge is the trestle of piles and beams used so extensively by railroads. Similar constructions

[214]

PLATE 186. Highway Arch at Saint Sauveur, France. A 138-foot span, 215 feet above the stream, completed in 1861. *Schérer & Marx, Engineers*. See "Grandes Voûtes," 1–27.

PLATE 187. Foot Bridge at Tuckahoe. *C. E. Wheeler, Designer, Westchester County Park Commission.*

PLATE 188. Rattan Suspension Bridge across the Tusta River, Cashmere, India

PLATE 189. The Kintai-Kyo, built in five timber arches of about 90-foot span, across the Nishiki-gawa in Iwakuni, Japan.

are used as falsework on which to build permanent bridges of stone, concrete or steel. Primitive suspension bridges were built of cables made of rattan or vines woven together (Plate 188). Such bridges are still in use in many countries.

* * * *

Concrete and steel have become the most important materials for the modern bridge. They are used either singly as plain concrete or structural steel; or in combination in the form of reinforced concrete. Plain concrete has properties similar to those of stone with this important difference: that natural stone has to be laboriously cut to shape, while concrete is made in a fluid or plastic condition, and can be moulded to any size or shape desired. This fundamental difference should be given expression in the structure, and the designer should avoid imitating in concrete the architectural forms of stonework. Projecting cornices and caps, brackets, turned balusters, and such familiar details of stone bridges may be meaningless in concrete, and should therefore be used with great caution. Such attempts at ornamentation may add considerably to the cost and actually detract from the appearance of the bridge. On account of the ease with which concrete can be moulded into elaborate forms, there is a great temptation to add details which are unnecessary. A study of hundreds of modern concrete bridges

PLATE 190. Traunfall and Traunbrücke. See Plate 297.

shows that the majority of them suffer from this cause. As a general rule, whenever there is doubt as to which of two architectural designs to use, it is better to choose the simpler.

Plain concrete, like stone masonry, is suitable only for compression and even in piers and heavy arches it is nearly always reinforced with at least a small amount of steel. When steel reinforcement is used the concrete is known as reinforced concrete; and the combination, by virtue of the steel, is capable of resisting tensile stresses as well as compression. The concrete protects from the elements the steel which lends it strength and it becomes as though by magic a material which may be used in almost any conceivable form. It is suitable for arches, beams, and trusses. In at least one case, it was used for a suspension bridge (Plate 191); but such a construction will probably not often be repeated. The suspension cable is, of course, made of steel encased in concrete.

There is no bridge building material which appeals as much to the imagination of the designer as reinforced concrete. It leaves him free to mould the bridge to any structural form which best suits the particular requirements of the site; and although it has been considerably abused, it is perfectly susceptible of beautiful architectural treatment. The choice between structural steel and reinforced concrete is a matter for careful consideration by an expert who

PLATE 191. Reinforced Concrete Suspension Bridge. Designed by E. Freyssinet

PLATE 192. Reinforced Concrete Girder Bridge at Gays Mills. *C. H. Kirch, Bridge Engineer, Wisconsin Highway Commission.*

understands all of the conditions. Reinforced concrete has been used in innumerable structural forms with spans varying from a few feet to the 590-foot spans near Brest, France. Much longer spans are possible.

Concrete is especially well suited to the construction of arch bridges, a type which has unusual architectural possibilities. Unfortunately, one of the most valuable properties of reinforced concrete has often been allowed to operate against the appearance of arch bridges. Because of its faculty for resisting tension, it is possible to build the arches narrower than the roadway and to cantilever part of the roadway, usually the sidewalks, out beyond the sides of the arch. This overhang, with its cantilever brackets, casts a strong shadow on the arch; and, in a great many cases, the effect is to ruin the appearance of an otherwise nicely proportioned bridge. It should be recognized that architecturally the projection of this overhang must be proportioned in the same manner as the cornice of a building; and that it bears a direct relation to the height of the bridge. The lower the bridge, the smaller should be the projection. It is safe to say that where appearance is important, the sidewalks should never be projected very far from the sides of the arch. Arches narrower than the roadway are usually adopted for economy. It will be found that, by careful designing, in most cases an objectionable overhang can be avoided without serious increase in cost.

The West Sixth Street Bridge at Racine, Wisconsin, is a modern design executed in reinforced concrete (Plates 193 to 197). Although there is no direct precedent for the design, its elements will be found in the early bridges. An attempt was made to express the structural form as simply as possible without meaningless ornament. The conventional cornice was

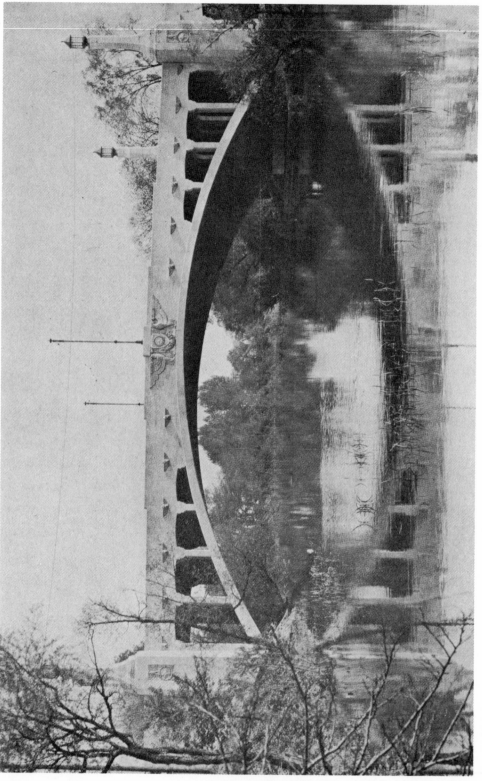

PLATE 193. West Sixth Street Bridge, Racine, Wis. *Charles S. Whitney and Joseph P. Schwada, Consulting Engineers; Eschweiler & Eschweiler, Associate Architects.*

PLATE 194. West Sixth Street Bridge, Racine

PLATE 195. West Sixth Street Bridge, Racine

PLATE 196. Faience Tile Panels and Bronze Name Plate, West Sixth Street Bridge, Racine

omitted entirely and gargoyles, also seen on ancient bridges, were used to mark the line of the sidewalk, and relieve the plain concrete spandrel walls.

The ornament at the center of the span with the trolley pole emphasizing the axis was suggested by the eighteenth century French bridges. Aside from the beveled edges and the mouldings of the pre-cast lamp standards, no mouldings at all were used in the concrete work. To reduce the severity of the structural lines, curved corbels were placed at the column heads. The gargoyles and center ornaments are of polychrome terra cotta. Inside the plain concrete parapets, above the sidewalks, were placed panels of colored faience tile which add greatly to the beauty of the bridge from the roadway.

PLATE 197. Driveway Span, West Sixth Street Bridge, Racine.

*　　*　　*　　*

Steel, which must be credited with making possible both the modern steel and the reinforced concrete bridge, has great strength in both tension and compression. It has one peculiarity which greatly influences its use; in compression its very strength is its weakness.

Because its strength permits the use of so little metal, the members are very slender and in compression they fail by bending or buckling sideways at a stress which is equal to about half of its breaking strength in tension. This requires that the members be built up in hollow shapes for stiffness and that they be braced at frequent intervals. For this reason steel can be used more economically in tension than in compression. The necessity for bracing of a member in compression makes the steel arch somewhat less satisfactory in appearance than the suspension bridge, although a steel arch is sometimes suitable where a suspension bridge would be entirely out of place. Steel has the advantages of strength and lightness, permanence when properly maintained, and adaptability to all types of spans.

In the long-span suspension bridge, steel finds its highest expression. No observer can escape the force of the grace and simplicity of such a structure. Each part has an obvious function and care need only be taken to see that each is properly expressed. In spite of its simplicity, this principle has been violated in important suspension bridges. The weight of the roadway is carried by the cables, so the stiffening trusses should be made as inconspicuous

PLATE 198. Drawing of the Proposed Liberty Bridge. 4500-foot span across the Entrance to New York Harbor. *Robinson & Steinman, Consulting Engineers; T. E. Blake, Associate Architect.*

as possible, to avoid the appearance of spanning from tower to tower with little or no assistance from the cables.

The towers receive the load of the span from the cables at their tops, and carry it directly to their bases. Since the towers are continuous past the roadway and the roadway is continuous past the towers, the intersection of tower and roadway should be recognized, but not

PLATE 199. Truss Railroad Bridge over the Rhone at Avignon, France

PLATE 200. Steel Arch Bridge over the Rhine at Bonn, Germany

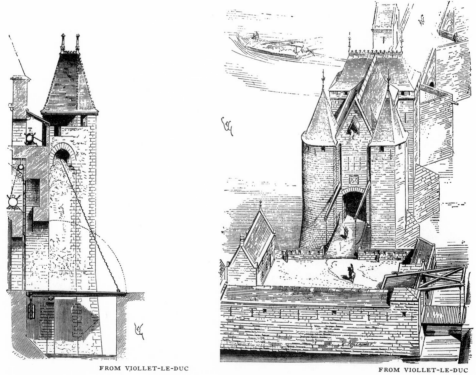

PLATE 201. Gate to the City of Villeneuve-sur-Yonne. Fourteenth century.

PLATE 202. Medieval Bridge End at Orléans, France.

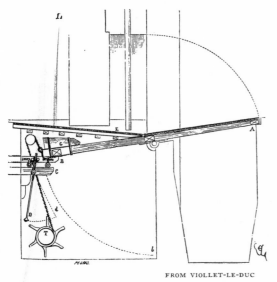

PLATE 203. Medieval Bascule with Raising Leaf.

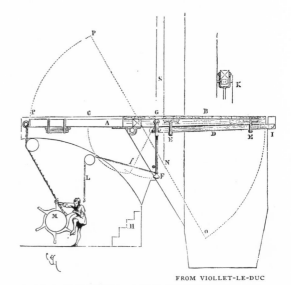

PLATE 204. Medieval Bascule with Lowering Leaf.

overemphasized. Comparatively little load is delivered to the towers at the roadway level by the stiffening trusses and it is a mistake to place great brackets under the trusses at the towers as was done on one large bridge.

An appearance of massive stability is appropriate for the anchorages where the cable ends are fastened.

*   *   *   *

In order to permit the passage of boats, it is frequently necessary to construct a bridge so that one span may be withdrawn, and many ingenious devices have been invented for this

purpose. There are three general types of modern movable bridges, the swing bridge which is balanced on a center pier and rotates about a vertical axis (Plate 395), the vertical lift which is raised vertically in a horizontal position, and the bascule which swings upward like the hinged cover of a box (Plate 206). There are many variations of each type.

The modern bascule bridge appears to have developed from the medieval drawbridge which was used for defense. The accompanying drawings, showing the mechanism of some

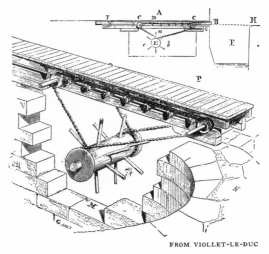

PLATE 205. Medieval Retractile Bridge

PLATE 206. Michigan Avenue Bascule Bridge, Chicago. Designed by the City of Chicago Bureau of Engineering. *H. E. Young, Engineer of Bridge Design; T. G. Pihlfeldt, Engineer of Bridges.*

early drawbridges, are reproduced from Viollet-le-Duc's "Dictionnaire Raisonné de l'Architecture," which gives an extremely interesting description of medieval fortifications.

The "pont levis" (Plate 201), a wooden platform raised with iron chains was used early in the fourteenth century for fortified gateways in France. Toward the end of the fifteenth century, when gun fire was introduced into warfare, these bridges were useless because the exposed chains could be shot away. Bascule bridges with no exposed mechanism were developed to overcome this difficulty. These were of two types, one with a leaf which raised up closing off the gateway (Plate 203); and another type, used in the east of France and along the Rhine, with a leaf which hinged down into the moat (Plate 204).

Another common type of medieval drawbridge was the retractile bridge which was put into service by sliding forward on rollers until the end projected across the moat or opening (Plate 205). This type was used in Italy and southern France much earlier than the fourteenth century. Many of them were built in Italy during the fifteenth century and in France after the introduction of artillery.

*   *   *   *

The sections which follow, contain pictures of bridges of many forms and sizes grouped together according to material and type. The majority of these are modern bridges. An attempt has been made to give credit to the designers and in some cases references are given to full technical descriptions. Some of these bridges have already been mentioned in the text. Beyond that, no criticism of the designs is given because it was thought best to allow the reader to analyze them and form his own opinion as to their merit. Architecture is not so positive as it is sometimes considered. To say "This is bad and that is good" is only to express personal taste unless the opinion is based on definite principles such as those which have been outlined.

The Bridge Engineer and Architect will find the following illustrations valuable for reference. The City Planner is interested in the Bridge as a link in the transportation system and as an ornament to the City. He will find many pictures of beautiful waterfront developments which should inspire improvements along waterways yet undeveloped. For the Landscape Architect there are views of attractive small bridges suitable for parks and private estates. No one can escape the spell of the Bridge, for there are all kinds of bridges to please all kinds of people.

PART II · SECTION II

BRIDGES OF WOOD

PLATE 207. Driveway Bridge, Garth Woods. *C. E. Wheeler, Designer, Westchester County Park Commission.*

[231]

PLATE 208. Driveway Bridge, Westchester County

PLATE 209. Foot Bridge at Hurley over the Thames

[232]

PLATE 210. Nuneham Bridge over the Thames

PLATE 211. Queen's College Bridge, Cambridge

PLATE 212. Kapellbrücke, Luzern, Switzerland. First built in 1333

PLATE 213. Spreuerbrücke, Luzern, Switzerland. First built in 1408. Destroyed by flood in 1566 and rebuilt in 1568.

PLATE 214. Spreuerbrücke, Luzern. "Toten-tanz" Paintings by Kasper Meglinger, 1626–36.

PLATE 215. Detail of Timber Framing in a Bridge at Aarberg. From "Altschweizerische Baukunst," by Dr. Roland Anheisser.

PLATE 216. Kapellbrücke, Luzern. Paintings in roof by Hans Heinrich Wegmann and his son in 1599.

PLATE 217. Covered Bridge over the Connecticut River

PLATE 218. Pont de Berne, Fribourg, Switzerland

PLATE 219. Taiko-bashi, Sumiyoshi, Sakai, Japan. Wooden bridge on stone piers

PLATE 220. Sacred Bridge at Nikko, Japan

[237]

PLATE 221. Benkei-Bashi, Tokyo, Japan

PLATE 222. Bridge in Peking, China

PLATE 223. Wooden Bridge at Bassano, Italy, said to have been designed by Palladio and Ferracina. Rebuilt in the nineteenth century.

PLATE 224. Thalkirchnerbrücke, Munich

[239]

PLATE 225. Cantilever Bridge at Paro Tong, Bhutan, India

PLATE 226. Cantilever Bridge at Chana, Bhutan, India

PART II · SECTION III

BRIDGES OF STONE

PLATE 227. Trinity College Bridge, Cambridge. Built by Essex in 1766

PLATE 228. Bridge at Chatsworth, England. About 1757

PLATE 229. Victoria Bridge, Leamington, England

PLATE 230. Sleights Bridge

PLATE 231. Penny Bridge, Caton, near Lancaster, England

PLATE 232. The Black Bridge, Blair Atholl

PLATE 233. Miller Bridge, Ambleside

PLATE 234. St. John's College Bridge, Cambridge. Possibly by Nicholas Hawksmore, a pupil of Wren. 1696.

PLATE 235. Pont de l'Empereur François, Prague. 1901. "Grandes Voûtes," I, p. 168

PLATE 236. Market Street Bridge, Harrisburg, Pa. Concrete arches faced with stone. *Ralph Modjeski and Frank M. Masters, Engineers; Paul P. Cret, Architect.*

PLATE 237. Market Street Bridge, Harrisburg, Pa.

PLATE 238. Arlington Memorial Bridge, Washington, D. C. Lieut-Col. C. O. Sherrill, Executive Officer, Arlington Memorial Bridge Commission. *W. J. Parsons, Consulting Engineer; McKim, Mead & White, Consulting Architects; John L. Nagle, Chief Designing Engineer.*

[249]

PLATE 239. Maximiliansbrücke, Munich, Germany. 1903–05. *Prof. Theodore Fischer, Architect; Saget & Woerner, Engineers.*

PLATE 240. Maximiliansbrücke, Munich

PLATE 241. Reichenbachbrücke, Munich. 1903. *Saget & Woerner, Engineers; Prof. Fr. von Thiersch, Architect.* "Grandes Voûtes," IV, p. 183.

[251]

PLATE 242. Max-Josefbrücke, Munich. 1902. Three-hinged stone arch. *Saget & Woerner, Engineers; Prof. Theodore Fischer, Architect.* "Grandes Voûtes," IV, p. 242.

PLATE 243. Max-Josefbrücke, Munich. Detail

PLATE 244. Max-Josefbrücke, Munich. Detail

[253]

PLATE 245. Wittelsbacherbrücke, with Memorial for Otto von Wittelsbach, Munich. 1905. *Saget & Woerner, Engineers; Prof. Theodore Fischer, Architect.* "Grandes Voûtes," IV, p. 199.

PLATE 246. Stone Bridge at Metz

PLATE 247. Corneliusbrücke, Munich. 1903. *Saget & Woerner, Engineers; Prof. von Thiersch, Architect.* "Grandes Voûtes," IV, p. 180.

PLATE 248. Ponte Umberto I, Turin, Italy

PLATE 249. Ponte Molino, Padua, Italy

PLATE 250. Ponte Solferino, Pisa, Italy

PLATE 251. Bridge at Poppi, Casentino, Italy

PLATE 252. Detail of Ponte Gregoriano, Tivoli, Italy

PLATE 253. Ponte Gregoriano, Tivoli, Italy

PLATE 254. Bridge at Gubbio, Umbria, Italy

PLATE 255. Bridge over the Nekar at Mannheim. 1908. *Gruen & Bilfinger, Engineers*. "Grandes Voûtes," IV, p. 206.

PLATE 256. Bridge at Nürnberg

PLATE 257. Park Avenue Bridge, Tuckahoe, N. Y. Stone-faced concrete bridge. Westchester County Park Commission, *Arthur G. Hayden, Designing Engineer; Harold M. Bowdoin, Architect.*

PLATE 258. Pelham Arch, Carrying 4-Track Main Line of N. Y., N. H. & H. Railroad over Hutchinson River Parkway. Stone-faced concrete arch. *Arthur G. Hayden, Designing Engineer.*

PLATE 259. East Third Street Bridge, Mount Vernon, N. Y. Stone-faced ribbed concrete bridge. *Arthur G. Hayden, Designing Engineer.*

PLATE 260. Palmer Avenue Bridge, Bronxville, N. Y. *Arthur G. Hayden, Designing Engineer; Charles W. Stoughton, Architect.*

PLATE 261. Ardsley Road Bridge, Scarsdale, N. Y. *Arthur G. Hayden, Designing Engineer; Charles W. Stoughton, Architect.*

[264]

PLATE 262. Bronx River Parkway Drive Bridge. *Guy Vroman, Designing Engineer; Carrere & Hastings, Architects.*

PLATE 263. Driveway Bridge, North White Plains. *Gilmore D. Clarke, Architect*

[265]

PLATE 264. Bridge in Peking, China

PLATE 265. Megane-Bashi, Nishi Otani, Kyoto, Japan

PLATE 266. Megane-Bashi. Detail

PLATE 267. Gokuraku-Bashi, Komyoji Temple, Kurodani, Kyoto, Japan

PHOTO BY BURR PHOTO CO.

PLATE 268. Canal Bridge, Shanghai, China

PHOTOS BY E. B. STROUT

PLATES 269 AND 269A. Bridge between Orr's Island and Bailey Island, Casco Bay, Maine. The Causeway is built of open stonework to permit the passage of tide-water. *Designed by Maine State Highway Commission; built by F. W. Carlton. Bath, Maine.*

[268]

PLATE 270. Viaduc de la Crueize, France. 82-foot spans, 206 feet high. 1879–83. "Grandes Voûtes," VI, p. 61.

PLATE 271. Viaduct near Fontpedrouse, France. 1908. 213 feet above stream. *Paul Séjourné, Engineer.* "Grandes Voûtes," V, p. 86.

PLATE 272. Viaduc du Piou. Between Séverac and Marvejol, France. 1877–79

PLATE 273. Roquefavour Aqueduct near Aix, France. 1841-47. About 1280 feet long and 272 feet high. Clear span of intermediate arches is 52 feet. Part of water supply canal from Durance to Marseilles, 57 miles long.

PLATE 274. Rheinbrücke at Eglisau

PLATE 275. Bridge at Solis, Switzerland. 1902. 138-foot span, 282 feet above stream. *Professor Hennings, Chief Engineer.* "Grandes Voûtes," I, p. 55.

PLATE 276. Waldlitobel Brücke, Austria. 1884. "Grandes Voûtes," II, p. 157

PLATE 277. Brombenzbrücke, Davos-Filisur-Bahn, Switzerland

PLATE 278. Bridge near Moulins-les-Metz, France. 1905. Stone-faced three-hinged concrete arches. *M. Blumhardt, Engineer.* "Grandes Voûtes," IV, p. 202.

PLATE 279. Pont Boucicaut at Verjux, France. 1890. *M. Tourtay, Engineer.* "Grandes Voûtes," III, p. 243.

PLATE 280. Viaduc de St. Chamas. P. L. M. Railroad between Marseilles and Avignon. "Grandes Voûtes," V, p. 57.

PART II · SECTION IV

BRIDGES OF CONCRETE

PHOTO BY C. S. WHITNEY

PLATE 281. Mound Cemetery Bridge, Racine, Wisconsin. Bedford Stone Railing. *Charles S. Whitney, Consulting Engineer.*

PLATE 282. San Diego Exposition Bridge. *Frank P. Allen, Jr., Engineer; Cram, Goodhue & Ferguson, Architects.* "Engineering News." 1915. Vol. I, p. 926.

PLATE 283. Pont de Zähringen, Fribourg, Switzerland. 1924. *Jaeger & Lusser, Engineers; Zublin & Cie, Contractors*

PLATE 284. Pont de Pérolles, Fribourg, Switzerland. 1924. *Jaeger & Lusser, Engineers; Frölich, Broillet & Genoud, Architects; Zublin & Cie, Contractors.*

PLATE 285. Pont de Pérolles, Fribourg, Switzerland

PLATE 286. Puente de Garrobillas, Spain, During Construction. *D. Cipriano Sabratreira, Engineer.*

PLATE 287. Grandfey Viaduct near Fribourg, Switzerland. *Adolf Bühler, Engineer.* See Plate 181

PLATE 288. Hlavkabrücke over the Moldau in Prague

PLATE 289. Manesbrücke over the Moldau in Prague

PLATE 290. *Connecticut Avenue Bridge, Washington, D. C. 1908. George S. Morrison and W. J. Douglas, Engineers*

PLATE 291. Tunkhannock Creek Viaduct, Lackawanna Railroad. 240 feet high. 1916. *Geo. J. Ray, Chief Engineer.* See Plate 184.

PLATE 292. Walnut Lane Bridge, Philadelphia. 1908. *George S. Webster, Chief Engineer; Henry H. Quimby, Assistant Engineer.* "Transactions," American Society of Civil Engineers, LXV, p. 423.

PLATE 293. Gmündertobelbrücke, near Teufen, Switzerland. 1908. 259-foot clear span. *Prof. E. Mörsch, Engineer; Froté, Westermann & Co., Contractor.*

PLATE 294. New and Old Bridges at Villeneuve-sur-Lot, France. 321-foot concrete arch. 1919. *E. Freyssinet, Engineer.* "Engineering News Record." 1924. II, p. 463.

PLATE 295. Hundwilertobelbrücke, Canton of Appenzell, Switzerland. 1925. Center span 236 feet. *A. Schläpfer, Kantonsingenieur; Ed. Zublin & Co., Contractors.*

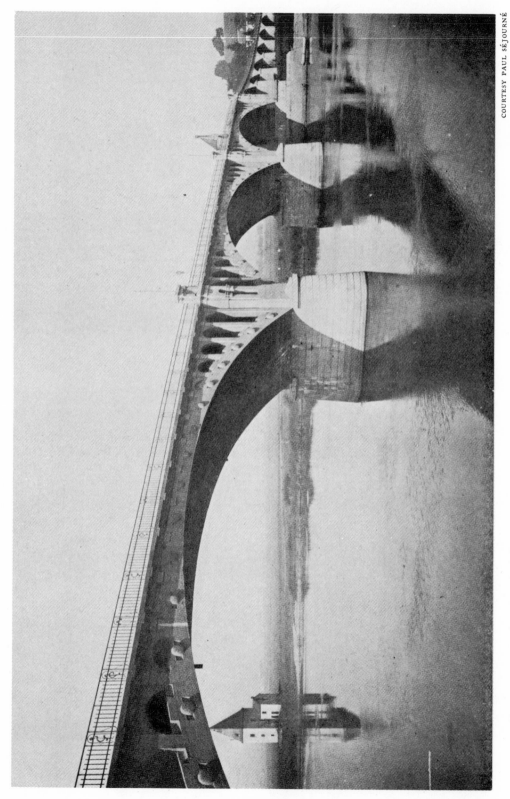

PLATE 296. Bridge over the Moselle at Schweich, Germany. 1906. Three 151-foot concrete arches. *B. Liebold & Cie, Engineers and Builders.* "Grandes Voûtes," III, p. 268.

PLATE 297. Traunbrücke at Gmünden, Austria. 1925. Two-hinged concrete arches of 233-foot span. *Dr. Fritz Emperger, Engineer.* "Génie Civil," 88, p. 369.

PLATE 298. Moselle Bridge at Mehring, Germany. 1904. Four 151-foot concrete arches. *B. Liebold & Cie, Engineers and Builders.* "Grandes Voûtes," III, p. 252.

PLATE 299. Street Bridge over the Elbe in Nymburk. 1913. Reinforced concrete arches, Monier system

PLATE 300. Harrison Avenue Viaduct, Scranton, Pa. 1922. Clear span of arch is 201 feet 8 inches.
A. B. Cohen, Designing and Consulting Engineer.

PLATE 301. Queen Victoria Bridge, Madrid. 1910. *J. Eugenio Ribera, Designer and Builder*

PLATE 302. Woodland Place Viaduct, White Plains, N. Y. *Guy Vroman, Designing Engineer; Palmer & Hornbostel, Architects.*

[293]

PLATES 303 AND 304. Bronze Plates, Washington Memorial Bridge

COURTESY F. W. CARPENTER

PLATE 305. Washington Memorial Bridge, Wilmington, Del. *F. W. Carpenter and B. H. Davis, Engineers; Vance Torbert, Architect.*

PLATE 306. Saw Mill River Parkway Drive Bridge, Yonkers, N. Y. *Arthur G. Hayden, Designing Engineer; Gilmore D. Clark, Architect.*

PLATE 307. Pont de Chaudron, Lausanne, Switzerland. 1905. *Designed by Professor Melan for Bellorini & Rochat, Builders.*

PLATE 308. Clarks Ferry Bridge over the Susquehanna River, Pennsylvania. *Frank M. Masters, Chief Engineer; Ralph Modjeski, Consulting Engineer; Paul Cret, Consulting Architect.*

PLATE 309. Clarks Ferry Bridge. General view before removal of old timber bridge

PLATE 310. Clarks Ferry Bridge. Detail

PLATE 311. Viaduc de Langweis, Switzerland. 1914. Concrete arch span of 315 feet. *Ed. Züblin et Cie, Designers and Builders.*

PHOTO BY EWING GALLOWAY

PLATE 312. Robert Street Bridge, Minneapolis, Minn. 1926. *Tolz, King & Day, Engineers and Architects.*

COURTESY GEORGE S. WEBSTER

PLATE 313. Bensalem Avenue Bridge, Philadelphia. 1920. Designed by Philadelphia Bureau of Surveys, *Geo. S. Webster, Chief Engineer.* "Engineering News Record," Vol. 85, pp. 531, 559, 619, 670, 810, 1006, 1024, 1104.

PLATE 314. Yaesu-Bashi, Tokyo, Japan. Started in 1924 by the Reconstruction Bureau

PLATE 315. Otter Creek Bridge, Eau Claire, Wis. Wisconsin Highway Commission, *C. H. Kirch, Bridge Engineer.*

PLATE 316. Mittlere Rheinbrücke, Basel, Switzerland. 1905. *A. G. Buss & Cie, Engineers; Faesch, Architect.*

PLATE 317. Bridge in Dlva. 1925. Concrete arches. Monier system

PHOTO BY WEHRLI A. G.

PLATE 318. Mittlere Rheinbrücke, Basel, Switzerland

PLATE 319. Pont Pasteur, Lyon, France. 1922. *C. Chalumeau, Engineer*

PLATE 320. Ponte del Risorgimento, Rome. 1911. A 328-foot span. *Hennebique, Engineer*

PLATE 321. 249-foot Span over the Spree at Treptow. *Dr. Ing. Fritz Emperger, Engineer*

PLATE 322. Highway Bridge at Saint-Pierre-du-Vauvray, France. 430-foot span. 1923. *E. Freyssinet, Engineer*. "Engineering News Record." 1924, II, p. 463.

PLATE 323. Bridge over the Vlara in Nemsova. 1924. Center span is 177 feet

PLATE 324. Street Bridge in Stankov. 1921. Center span about 110 feet

PLATE 325. Bridge over the Oued Saf-Saf, Algeria. Seven spans of 82 feet. *Henry Lossier, Engineer*

PLATE 326. Bridge over the Saone at Thoissey, France. Spans are 170.6 feet, 203.4 feet and 170.6 feet. Reinforced concrete. Hennebique system.

PLATE 327. Erhardtbrücke, Munich

PLATE 328. Girder Bridge over the Ill in Alsace. *Ed. Zublin & Cie, Engineers and Builders*

PLATE 329. Madison Avenue Bridge, Madison, N. J. 1915. *G. J. Ray, Chief Engineer, D., L. & W. Railroad.*

[308]

PLATE 330. Girder Bridge in Neenah, Wis. Wisconsin Highway Commission, *C. H. Kirch, Bridge Engineer*.

PLATE 331. James Park Bridge, Madison, N. J. 1915. *G. J. Ray, Chief Engineer, D., L. & W. Railroad*

PLATE 332. Brick Church Viaduct, East Orange, N. J. 1923. *G. J. Ray, Chief Engineer, D., L. & W. Railroad.*

PLATE 333. Bronx River Parkway Drive Bridge at Scarsdale, N. Y. *Arthur G. Hayden, Designing Engineer; Delano & Aldrich, Architects.*

PLATE 334. Bronx River Parkway Drive Bridge at Scarsdale, N. Y.

PLATE 335. Interesting Pier Design for Girder Bridge Crossing Land Subject to Floods

[311]

PART II · SECTION V

BRIDGES OF STEEL

PLATE 336. Crooked River Arch, Oregon Trunk Railway. *Ralph Modjeski, Consulting Engineer*

PLATE 337. Hudson River Suspension Bridge at New York, between Fort Washington and Fort Lee. The span is 3500 feet and the towers are 650 feet high, nearly one hundred feet higher than the Washington Monument. See also plate 2. *O. H. Ammann, Chief Engineer; Cass Gilbert, Consulting Architect.*

PLATE 338. Preliminary Study of Hudson River Bridge, New York

PLATE 339. Preliminary Study of Development of New York Approach to Hudson River Bridge. Separate driveways from Riverside Drive provided for on- and off-bound traffic to avoid crossing of traffic lanes.

PLATE 340. Hudson River Bridge. Approach Drive crossing Riverside Park south of the Bridge. Preliminary study.

PLATE 341. Philadelphia-Camden Suspension Bridge over the Delaware River. Opened to traffic July 3, 1926. 1750-foot span. Board of Engineers: *Ralph Modjeski, Chairman; George S. Webster and Laurence A. Ball. Paul P. Cret, Consulting Architect.*

PLATE 342. Philadelphia-Camden Bridge. Detail of Anchorage

PLATE 343. Philadelphia-Camden Bridge. Detail of Tower

PLATE 344. Philadelphia-Camden Bridge.
Detail of Anchorage.

PLATE 345. Philadelphia-Camden Bridge.
Detail of Anchorage Pylon from Roadway.

PLATE 346. Manhattan Bridge, New York City. 1909. Span length 1470 feet. City of New York Department of Plants and Structures. *Carrere & Hastings, Consulting Architects.*

PLATE 347. Elizabeth Bridge, Budapest. 1905. *A. Czechelius, Engineer; M. Nagy, Architect*

PLATE 348. Old Chain Suspension Bridge, Budapest. 1849. *W. T. Tierney Clarke, Engineer*

COURTESY MASCH. AUGSBURG-NÜRNBERG

PLATE 349. Self-Anchoring Suspension Bridge, Cologne. 1915. Span 604.9 feet. *Maschinenfabrik Augsburg-Nürnberg A.G., Designers and Builders.* "Engineering News Record," 70, p. 845.

PLATE 350. Suspension Bridge at Cologne. Detail

PLATE 351. Seventh Street Bridge, Pittsburgh, Pa. Ninth Street Bridge under construction. 1926
County of Allegheny Department of Public Works. *V. R. Covell, Chief Engineer of Bridges.*

PLATE 352. Bridge over the Moldau in Prague. 1908

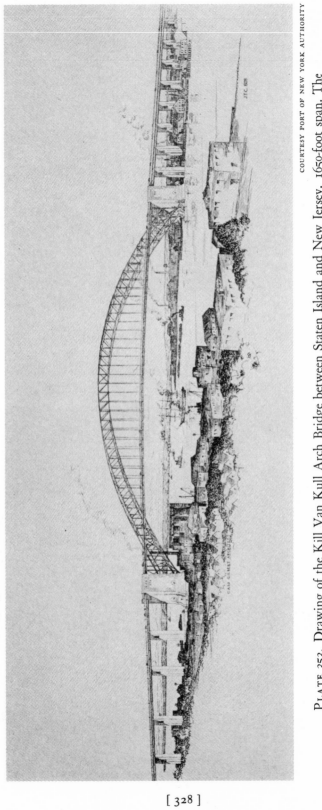

PLATE 353. Drawing of the Kill Van Kull Arch Bridge between Staten Island and New Jersey. 1650-foot span. The masonry abutment towers are nicely designed to give an appearance of stability to the arch without over-emphasis which would interrupt the continuous line of the roadway. *O. H. Ammann, Chief Engineer of Bridges, Port of New York Authority; Cass Gilbert, Architect.*

PLATE 354. Kill Van Kull Bridge. Drawing of Abutment

PLATE 355. Naniwa-Bashi, Tokyo

PLATE 356. Frankfurt-am-Main, Germany

PLATE 357. Dresden, Germany

PLATE 358. Longfellow Bridge across the Charles River between Boston and Cambridge. Built under Cambridge Bridge Commission, 1908. *William Jackson, Chief Engineer; Edmund Wheelwright, Architect.*

PLATE 359. Longfellow Bridge, Boston. Detail

PLATE 360. Pont Alexandre, Paris

PLATE 361. Levallois Bridge, Paris. 1923. Built by Ateliers Moisant-Laurent-Savey

PLATE 362. Pont d'Ainay, Lyon. 1899. *H. Girardon, Chief Engineer*

PLATE 363. Pont la Feuillée, Lyon. 1912. *C. Chalumeau, Engineer*

Plate 364. New Steel Span of High Bridge, New York, with Washington Bridge in Background

Plate 365. Spillway Bridges, Croton Dam, New York

PLATE 366. Washington Bridge, New York City. 1889

PLATE 367. Coblenz, Germany

PLATE 368. Marble Canyon Bridge over the Colorado River, Arizona. 1928. 616-foot span, 467 feet above the river. Arizona State Highway Commission. *R. A. Hoffman, Bridge Engineer; L. C. Lashmet, Designing Engineer.*

PLATE 369. Park Avenue Bridge at Grand Central Station, New York

PLATE 370. Highway Arch of 330-foot Span over Crooked River Gorge, Oregon. Oregon State Highway Commission, *C. B. McCullough, Bridge Engineer.*

PHOTO BY JUDGES, LTD.

PLATE 371. Stoke Bridge, Ipswich

COURTESY OBERBÜRGERMEISTER, COLOGNE

PLATE 372. South Bridge, Cologne. 1910. Central Span 541 feet

PLATE 373. Hohenzollernbrücke, Cologne. 1911. Central Span 551 feet

PLATE 374. Hell Gate Arch of the New York Connecting Railway, New York. 1916. Span 1000 feet. *Gustav Lindenthal, Engineer.*

PLATE 375. Rhine Bridge at Düsseldorf, Germany

PLATE 376. Pont de Chaulnes, Chemin de fer du Nord, France. *Schneider & Cie, Builders*

PLATE 377. Forth Bridge, Scotland. 1890. The main spans are 1710 feet long. *Designed by Sir Benjamin Baker*

PLATE 378. Highway Bridge over the Mosel at Wehlen. 1926. *Maschinenfabrik Augsburg-Nürnberg A. G., Builders.*

PLATE 379. Quebec Cantilever Bridge. Completed in 1917. Span length of 1800 feet, exceeded only by the Detroit-Windsor and the Hudson River Bridges now under construction. Board of Engineers: *C. N. Monsarrat, Chief Engineer; Ralph Modjeski, C. C. Schneider and H. P. Borden.*

PLATE 380. Franz-Josefs Brücke, Budapest, Hungary

PLATE 381. Elizabeth-Howland Hook Bridge across the Arthur Kill. Central span 672 feet. Port of New York Authority, *O. H. Ammann, Bridge Engineer; York & Sawyer, Architects.*

PLATE 382. Outerbridge Crossing over Arthur Kill. Central span 750 feet. Port of New York Authority. *O. H. Ammann, Bridge Engineer; York & Sawyer, Architects.*

PLATE 383. Pont de l'Homme de la Roche, Lyon, France. 1912. *A. Auric and C. Chalumeau, Engineers.*

PLATE 384. Railroad Bridge at Cologne, Germany. 1859.

PLATE 385. Friedens Bridge over the Danube, Vienna, Austria. 1926. Built by Waagner-Biro A. G.

PLATE 386. Pont de Cubzac over the Dordogne, France

PLATE 387. Railroad Bridge at Mayence, Germany

PLATE 388. McKinley Bridge, St. Louis, Mo. *Ralph Modjeski, Consulting Engineer*

PLATE 389. Highway Bridge of 169-foot 3-inch span at Gelsenkirchen, Germany. 1912. *Friedrich Krupp, Builder.*

PLATE 390. Highway Bridge over the Danube at Vienna, Austria. 1919. Plate girder spans 108 feet three inches. *Waagner-Biro A. G., Builder.*

[351]

PLATE 391. Friedrich Ebert Bridge, Mannheim, Germany. *Maschinenfabrik Augsburg-Nürnberg A. G., Builders.*

PLATE 392. Bridge over Bank Street, Prudential Life Insurance Buildings, Newark. *Cass Gilbert, Architect.*

PLATE 393. Bridge over Halsey Street, Prudential Life Insurance Buildings, Newark. *Cass Gilbert, Architect.*

PLATE 394. Transporter Bridge across Entrance to Harbor, Marseilles, France

PLATE 395. Le Pont Tournant, Military Port of Brest, France

PLATE 396. Bascule of Tower Bridge, London

PLATE 397. Kilbourn Avenue Bascule Bridge, Milwaukee. 1929. Designed by Bureau of Bridges and Buildings, City of Milwaukee. *Manuel Cutler, Bridge Engineer.*

PLATE 398. Kilbourn Avenue Bascule Bridge, Milwaukee. 1929. Designed by Bureau of Bridges and Buildings, City of Milwaukee. *Manuel Cutler, Bridge Engineer.*

PLATE 399. Michigan Avenue Bascule Bridge, Chicago. See Plate 206

PLATE 400. Perspective Drawing of University Bridge, Philadelphia. Double-leaf bascule with 100-foot clear channel. Designed by the Bureau of Engineering, City of Philadelphia. *John A. Vogleson, Chief Engineer; Paul P. Cret, Consulting Architect.*

INDEX

NOTE: *References to text are indicated with* t *thus:* t191. *All others are illustrations.*